# Namibia
## reclaiming the people's health

Edited by
Tim Lobstein
and
The Namibia Support Committee Health
Collective

September 1984

First published September 1984.
Copyright © AON Publications, Namibia Support Committee,
P.O. Box 16, London NW5 2LW.

ISBN 0 947905 01 4 paperback
ISBN 0 947905 00 6 hardback

Cover design by Carol Brickley/Red Lion Setters
Designed and Typeset by Red Lion Setters, London WC1.
Printed in Great Britain by The Russell Press Limited, Nottingham.
Marketed and Promoted by Ultra Violet Enterprises, London N5.
Distributed by Third World Publications,
151 Stratford Road, Birmingham B11 1RD (021-773 6572).

# Contents

306642

# Namibia

International boundaries
Roads
Perennial rivers
Seasonal rivers
• Towns, villages
★ Dams
+++++ Railways

# Acknowledgements

Most of this book is derived from papers given at the International Seminar on Health in Namibia, organised by the Namibia Support Committee in co-operation with the SWAPO Department of Health and Social Welfare, and held in London in October 1983. The Seminar was sponsored by the United Nations Council for Namibia and attracted representatives from over thirty aid agencies and solidarity groups, in addition to observers from the International Committee on Southern Africa, the United Nations High Commission for Refugees, the United Nations Council for Namibia and the World Health Organisation. More material for the book came from the workshops and discussions held during the Seminar, from material written by people attending the Seminar and other contributions through the Namibia Support Committee Health Collective. We cannot name here all the people attending the Seminar nor attribute all the comments that were made. Instead we list the main contributors, whose material formed the basis of the section shown, and express our immense gratitude to all the unnamed people who have helped make the book what it is. (A set of the papers presented to the Seminar and a summary of the proceedings may be purchased direct from the Namibia Support Committee for £10.)

We acknowledge with thanks the material included in Chapter Nine which we have adapted from David Werner and Bill Bower's *Helping Health Workers Learn* (see Appendix). We are also grateful for the otherwise unacknowledged work done for this book by Vanda Playford, Mike Murphy and Terry Shott of the Namibia Support Committee Health Collective.

Lastly we want to express our thanks to the financial sponsors who have helped ensure that this book could be published and the material of the Seminar reach a far wider audience. The sponsors include the United Nations Council for Namibia. We are indebted to Red Lion Setters for their help in designing and typesetting this book.

## Main Contributors

Chapter 1: Tim Lobstein and The Namibia Support Committee Health Collective.
Chapter 2: Brian Hackland and The Namibia Support Committee Health Collective.

Chapter 3: Barbara König and The SWAPO Womens Solidarity Campaign.

Chapter 4: David Sanders (Department of Paediatrics and Child Health, University of Zimbabwe Medical School, Harare, Zimbabwe).

Chapter 5: David Werner (c/o The Hesperian Foundation, Palo Alto, California 94302, USA).

Chapter 6, Part 1: Godfrey Walker and Gill Walt (both at The London School of Hygiene and Tropical Medicine, London WC1).

Chapter 6, Part 2: Steve Woodhouse and Isabel de Zoysa (London School of Hygiene and Tropical Medicine, London WC1).

Chapter 6, Part 3: Zef Ebrahim and Pam Zinkin (both at The Institute of Child Health, London WC1).

Chapter 6, Part 4: Sue Hunt (Namibia Support Committee Health Collective) and Rene Loewenson (London School of Hygiene and Tropical Medicine, London WC1).

Chapter 6, Part 5: Martin Hobdell (Department of Community Dental Health, Trinity College, University of Dublin, Eire).

Chapter 6, Part 6: Vic Finkelstein.

Chapter 7: Neil Andersson (London School of Hygiene and Tropical Medicine, London WC1) and Arthur Pickering (Namibia Refugee Project).

Chapter 8: Carol Barker (Nuffield Centre for Health Service Studies, Leeds) and Diana Melrose (Oxfam Public Affairs Unit, Oxford).

Chapter 9: David Werner (c/o The Hesperian Foundation).

Chapter 10: Tim Lobstein and the Namibia Support Committee Health Collective.

Appendix compiled by Tim Lobstein and the Namibia Support Committee Health Collective.

Index compiled by Dave Simmonds.

## SWAPO Representatives at the Seminar

| | |
|---|---|
| Vizcaya Amtenya | Vicky Ashikoto |
| Erica Ndiyepa | Jacob Hannai |
| Iyambo Indongo | Shapua Kaukungua |
| Erasmus Nganyone | Peter Manning |
| Airah Schikwambi | |

# Foreword

## The Effects of Colonialism on Health

*Dr Iyambo Indongo*
*Secretary for Health and Social Welfare*
*SWAPO of Namibia*

Health Services in illegally occupied Namibia are adversely affected by colonialism with its apartheid system, and by the current war. The experience of newly liberated nations in Africa and elsewhere in the developing world demonstrates that health services, administered by people who had no African's interests at heart, were very bad during colonialism and improved steadily after independence. In Namibia, colonial administration is based on racial discrimination. So, too, health care is racially discriminating, urban oriented and almost exclusively curative, leading to worse health for the blacks who are discriminated against. The war that is going on there is one of the bloodiest for those whose skin colour is dark.

Health services are run by the illegal administration, churches and, to a lesser extent, mines and private practitioners. Fragmentation of the administrative framework engenders contradictions and problems in implementation of health programmes. Those programmes run by the colonialists are segregated, while others, for instance those run by the church, are not. This contrast causes friction between these organisations and sometimes results in drastic cutbacks of subsidies or closure of church health facilities.

Registration of births and deaths among blacks is non-existent, yet there has been unbroken registration of beef cattle owned by boers on large-scale farms. Registration of black males occurs when they are grown enough to sell their labour. Like beasts of burden, black men attract the attention of masters only when they are bidden for at auctions where they are registered for contract labour and taxation. African women and children are not normally registered at all.

In a situation like this, it is virtually impossible to know what the health status of the population is, especially as figures from South African documents are merely distorted estimates that are meant to mislead those who do not take them with a grain of salt.

SWAPO of Namibia has two main objectives. Firstly it aims to provide *health care* for all those Namibians displaced by the war and now living in the *Namibia Health and Education Centres* which are situated in Angola and Zambia, as well as to render service to combatants of the People's Liberation Army of Namibia, SWAPO's military wing, and our civilian population in 'operational areas'.

The second objective for SWAPO is to devise *health plans for an independent Namibia*, based on practical experience gained during the last 23 years, since the foundation of SWAPO. We have also learned a lot from the experience of former sister Liberation Movements (now ruling parties) such as MPLA, FRELIMO, ZANU and others, which devised their health policy during their struggles for freedom.

## SWAPO's Health Care

Intensification of the liberation war waged by the people of Namibia against the racist army of South Africa, compounded by the defeat of the Portuguese by the liberation movements in Angola and Mozambique, and the victory of ZANU in Zimbabwe, caused a terrible shock to the racist regime in Pretoria. In reaction Pretoria resorted to sordid suppression through vicious acts of terror.* The victims are mostly innocent civilians who were suspected of sympathising with or supporting SWAPO. In spite of all these atrocities and violations of human rights aimed at the extermination of Namibians, and despite numerous United Nations Resolutions calling for unconditional withdrawal of its brutal racist army from Namibia, South Africa still enjoys economic, military and many other forms of support from the Western and North American countries. We have appealed to these countries to join the rest of the human race in rejection of all manner of support to the apartheid regime. This could compel it to comply with the international community's demands for the immediate implementation of the U.N. Security Council Resolution 435.

The wanton killing and all other barbaric acts against innocent civilians forced many to flee the country to live in exile in neighbouring countries. Even those who have succeeded in crossing the borders are not safe. They are being pursued, killed or captured. Those killed during the Oshatotwa raid in Zambia in 1976, and the Cassinga Massacre of 1978 in Angola, were such arrivals. Those captured have disappeared or been thrown into concentration camps like Hardap Dam near Mariental, in Kobabis and other places.

* Just prior to the seminar at which this foreword was delivered vivid evidence of Pretoria's activities was broadcast on British television: *The Devil's Circle*, Channel 4, October 5th 1983.

In *Namibia Health and Education Centres* located in Zambia and Angola, as in Namibia itself, determinants of illness and deaths are communicable, parasitic conditions and malnutrition. Poor sanitary conditions, inadequate water supply and overcrowding aggravate other poverty-linked diseases that lead to high infant and maternal death rates. Since the earliest foundation of health services in the Centres it has been apparent that the determinants of health stretch well beyond medical care. Basic needs identified were food, clothing and shelter, as well as essential social services provided by and for the community, e.g. education and health facilities, water supply, sanitation, transport etc. Indeed, in countries where it has been possible for people to settle with minimum threats of air raids and to build shelters, have access to adequate water supply, as well as to grow some foodstuffs, there has been a steady improvement in health status. For example in some areas infant mortality dropped from over 100 per 1,000 live births to 41 per 1,000.

## Health Plans for an Independent Namibia

To start with, it was extremely difficult to plan without data from Namibia. Since we live in exile, it was and still is impossible to conduct a survey there, because two-thirds of the country is under martial law. This includes virtually all the black reserves (so-called homelands). However, in 1980 a Country Health Programming exercise was carried out in Lusaka in collaboration with the World Health Organisation (WHO). This was made possible by obtaining, through various sources, data (albeit often out of date and unreliable) from Namibia. The participants in the exercise gained valuable theoretical experience in planning, and drew up a tentative health plan. The exercise is due to be repeated as part of on-going planning and training. At the Lusaka meeting the goals of the health policy of SWAPO were formulated. Principal among these was the acceptance of the WHO goal of 'Health for all by the year 2000 through Primary Health Care'. The meeting accepted the strategy of community participation in shaping and improving health care, a common factor between the SWAPO Constitution and the long-term objectives defined by WHO. A commitment was made to break with the prevailing racial orientation in health services, as with the curative urban orientation.

The following long-term objectives were made explicit:

(a)  to create an equally distributed service for all Namibians, irrespective of race, sex, colour, religion and social status;

(b) to emphasise preventive strategy, placing emphasis on the needs of the rural population;

(c) to supply free medical services for all and to terminate the present exploitative private practice.

The short-term objectives were outlined to overcome the immediate needs of the post-independent period:

(a) to overcome the post-independent manpower shortage within three years (mostly expected outflow of existing medical staff);

(b) to maintain the present pre-independent level of health services in the urban areas;

(c) to improve and extend the coverage by the health service into the rural areas.

In conclusion, I wish to appeal to all agencies, governments and solidarity groups who are supporters of the oppressed people in Namibia and Southern Africa as a whole, to increase their material support for the struggle.

*October 1983*

# Statements of SWAPO's policies

## 1. Extracts from the SWAPO Constitution

'SWAPO will work towards the creation of a non-exploitative and non-oppressive classless society.'

'SWAPO will combat reactionary tendencies of individualism, tribalism, racism, sexism and regionalism.'

'SWAPO will establish in Namibia a democratic, secular government founded upon the will and participation of all the Namibian people.'

## 2. Statement from SWAPO's Political Programme on Health and Social Services

'OUR health and social services programme in an independent Namibia shall strive for preventive as well as for curative medicine for all the citizens along the following lines:

'(a)  there shall be comprehensive, free medical services in an independent and democratic Namibia;
(b)  there shall be hospitals and clinics in every district of our country;
(c)  there shall be nurseries and clinics in every community for the working people and their families;
(d)  there shall be health education centres for preventive medicine and family planning;
(e)  there shall be training institutions for the training of medical and para-medical personnel;
(f)  there shall be rehabilitation centres for disabled and infirm persons; and
(g)  there shall be an International Red Cross society.

'THE living and working conditions of the workers in Namibia have deteriorated to such an extent that we have reached a stage of class struggle between the People's Liberation Army of Namibia (PLAN, SWAPO's military wing) and the racist South African army. This is not a stated intention, it is a practice. The early implementation of the United Nations Resolution 435 and the independence of Namibia would help to defuse this explosive situation; when measures can be taken to prevent the perpetuation of inequality in the health sector and provide a comprehensive national health care which will be acceptable, appropriate, accessible, economical and permit increasing involvement of the community in health decision making.

'The prevailing disease pattern and social inequality in health care cannot be altered for the better under the existing social order. The situation in Southern Africa in general and in Namibia in particular is dangerous and explosive.'

# Preface

## Randolph Vigne

*Honorary Secretary, Namibia Support Committee*

The long struggle for freedom in Namibia has entailed great suffering for the people of that country. For the past 15 years, the Namibian Support Committee has campaigned in Britain in support of the Namibian liberation movement, SWAPO, and against the illegal South African occupation. As part of its campaign, the Committee has striven to build political, diplomatic and material support for SWAPO, both to promote the struggle and to provide some relief to those suffering the effects of war, repression, political terror and refugee exile.

The Committee was formed in part in response to the 1968 trial in Pretoria, South Africa, of SWAPO activists and freedom fighters resulting from the first major military clash with South African occupation forces at Ongulumbashe in 1966. To meet the needs of the worsening situation in the mid-1970s, the Committee set up a Health Collective of professional health workers and volunteers. The Collective has since designed, financed and packed many hundreds of medical 'kits' for use among the 90,000 Namibian refugees in the SWAPO Health and Education Centres in Angola and Zambia, and also by SWAPO in Namibia itself. It has also supplied emergency aid, such as to the victims of South African aggression in the massacre at Kassinga in May 1978, and has (jointly with SWAPO Women's Council and the SWAPO Women's Solidarity Campaign) provided both a Landrover ambulance and a Maternity and Child Clinic, as well as other material and medical aid to the refugee settlements.

These and other initiatives have cost large sums of money, which the Health Collective has raised in co-operation with solidarity groups in the Netherlands, France and elsewhere, and from aid agencies, churches, individuals, and students and trades unions in Britain.

In accord with SWAPO's dual role leading the fight for the freedom of Namibia and as an architect of a genuine national independence after liberation, the Health Collective has been privileged to concern itself not only with the needs of Namibians as victims of South African colonialism and military repression today, but also with the plans for the establishment of the integrated national health system for an independent Namibia. Such a system will have to deal with the gross inequalities, neglect and injustices of the South African-imported apartheid system, itself only the last stage of a century of colonial exploitation.

To address itself to this great task, the historic International Seminar on Health in Namibia held at the City University, London, on 14-16 October 1983, the contents of which formed the basis of this book, was convened by the Namibian Support Committee in co-operation with the SWAPO Department of Health and Social Welfare. Organized by the Health Collective and supported by the United Nations Council for Namibia, the Seminar brought together SWAPO health workers with key representatives from aid agencies, solidarity groups, health organizations, trade unions, medical schools and the World Health Organization.

An achievement of the Seminar was to cover, through the contributions of those participating, an exhaustive range of themes in both written papers for the plenary sessions and workshop discussions on specific topics. Inevitably, participants were preoccupied with the terrible problems of war and its military and civilian victims, of population displacement and other consequences of political repression, and with SWAPO's health policy for a free Namibia, in its widest implications. The Seminar had, indeed, described its brief as 'Working Towards Health care in an Independent Namibia' including the realities of today and the blueprints for tomorrow.

The high quality of the presentations and discussions can be judged from the material now published here. Those who made the International Seminar of 1983 the success it was, in particular the Namibia Support Committee Health Collective and the SWAPO Department of Health and Social Welfare, can hope with some confidence that this book will spread the message of the participants: that the SWAPO government of an independent Namibia will need the support of all those concerned with health care throughout the world in its task of reclaiming the people's health.

# 1

# Introduction

There is a village in rural Namibia where a small girl called Ndalila, barely a year old, is lying on a blanket on the floor of her mother's hut. Ndalila is dying. Her mother has left her with her elder sister to go and see a traditional healer.

Ndalila has had diarrhoea for several weeks. Diarrhoea is common in the family and they have treated her with the usual mixture of herbs and clay. Her elder sister is sleeping on another blanket next to the child. Ndalila starts to whimper quietly, crying but without any tears. Her sister wakes and lifts her up: another wet, soiled blanket needs cleaning. She picks up the blanket, and the limp, loose body of the child, and carries them to the bucket outside.

Ndalila has a story which is told and re-told the world over in many forms about many, many children. Pictures of these stories are seen on televisions and in newspapers throughout the rich industrial west. Why is Ndalila dying? She has diarrhoea, comes the obvious answer. But why has she got diarrhoea? From an organism in the water. But why hasn't everybody got diarrhoea, then? Because Ndalila is malnourished and far more susceptible to infection. What is more, the diarrhoea itself means that she may have been losing 500 or more calories every day in her stools, making her lack of nutrition even worse. And most critical of all is that she has lost almost all the fluid her body can tolerate: she is severely dehydrated.

Deaths of Africans are rarely registered in Namibia and no death certificate will be needed for Ndalila. But if one were to be completed for her, what should be written for the cause of death? The dehydration was caused by the diarrhoea, but diarrhoea does not in itself kill. It may not even seriously incapacitate a well-fed child. What then is causing Ndalila's death? Malnourishment. But why is Ndalila chronically malnourished? Perhaps her mother did not know what to feed Ndalila – should we write on the certificate 'death from ignorance'?

In fact most mothers do know what a child needs, but not all mothers are in a position to supply what is wanted. For Ndalila's family, not only was water in short supply – encouraging the spread of infections – but food was even harder to come by. Should we write, then, 'death from poverty'? But why couldn't the family grow food? The weather was bad that year, with little rain. There had been long periods of curfew. Many of the men were away working in the mines, or looking for jobs or fighting in the war. The women worked together tending the surviving crops on the little land they had between them. 'Death from war'? 'Death from lack of jobs'? 'Death from lack of land'?

Even at this late stage of Ndalila's illness she might be treated success-fully with intravenous fluids if not with oral rehydration. Why hasn't she been taken to a clinic? Because the nearest clinic is several days' travelling away, and there would be the lost production to consider, and the cost of transport and the clinic fee. Few children in her condition had survived the journey, let alone recovered. But why are there no clinics nearer to this village? The war had closed some clinics, but in Ndalila's area no clinic has ever been built. Why? Because the rural health budget is very small. But why is there such a low priority for rural services in the national budget? Perhaps we should write 'death from social neglect'? But what is the budget spent on? Who benefits from the present distribution of the health budget?

If one asks why over and over again then the picture may gradually clear, and the reasons for Ndalila's death be seen to be material reflections of the political and economic organisation of the country. Taking a story such as this and repeatedly probing into the reasons why it has happened borrows very greatly from the teaching methods developed by David Werner – the *BUT WHY?* method – which we discuss in much more detail in Chapter 10.

The purpose of taking this story and exploring its implications here is to demonstrate to the readers of this book why we cannot simply talk about 'Health in Namibia' without also talking about social and political organisa-tion. We cannot talk about diseases and their treatment without looking at their causes, and we cannot look at their causes without asking how best they can be prevented. Very soon we find we cannot talk about programmes of preventive health without talking about the political control of resources. Then in turn we ask how those resources are distributed and to whom?

This book does not aim to be a record of the situation in Namibia in the late 1970s and early 1980s. Instead it takes as its starting point the vision of an independent Namibia and then proceeds to look at the sorts of problems that are likely to be encountered. It does this largely by examining the prob-lems that other underdeveloped and newly independent countries have faced in other parts of the world including Southern Africa – and particu-larly Mozambique and Zimbabwe – and looks at the radical ways in which these problems can be tackled.

There are a number of themes which run through this book recurring in different forms in different contexts. Where they emerge they speak for themselves, but we would like to draw attention to them at this stage. Some of the themes apply to a discussion of health in any country in the world, others take on a special importance in the context of Namibia's struggle for freedom from occupation, from oppression and from apartheid.

First, health reflects social relationships as much as it reflects biological function. The way health is produced – both by the formal health services producing medical treatments, and by individuals caring for themselves and (particularly in the case of women) for their families – determines the patterns of disease shown in the community. The social structures that produce health care are part of the social production of all goods and services, all 'wealth'. If these social structures are exploitative, if they are racist, if they are sexist, then the resulting pattern of diseases will show more suffering and ill-health among the exploited, among the oppressed races and among the oppressed sex. And this is not a relative statement – we do not mean that more privileged groups simply enjoy better health than less privileged groups but rather we mean that the introduction of an exploitative, oppressive social structure actually worsens the health of those who are exploited and oppressed. The early colonisers and settlers at the forefront of imperialism claimed that they were bringing spiritual and material wealth to the 'uncivilised indigenate'. In fact they brought new and devastating diseases and material poverty of a form never before experienced. For the descendants of those who were colonised, it has meant a significant and long-lasting decline in their overall health.

Just as the economic and social conditions determine the health of individuals and of a class, so their health in turn determines their ability to interact with their material and social world. Those who are plagued by illness, who suffer recurring episodes of malaria or bilharzia, whose children need frequent nursing, whose brother has polio or whose sister cannot space her child-bearing can all bear witness to the loss of earnings and loss of production ill-health brings. Their increasing poverty leads to increasing ill-health. Those with the greatest need of good health have the least chance of attaining it.

Health is thus a highly political concern. Health is everyone's daily practice. It is people's own attempts to meet their own needs and the needs of their dependants – every mother a health worker! Access to health resources means more than just access to a nearby clinic or hospital. It means access to the basic requirements for sustaining health: food, water, housing, knowledge. Access to these resources depends on their distribution, a distribution based ultimately on political practice. Ultimately a professional health worker, serving the needs of the majority of the people, will need to act politically. Ultimately health workers, in the name of health, will need to confront land owners and food producers, confront mine owners and industrialists, confront professional politicians, governments, armies, and privilege wherever it appears. Ultimately health workers may have to confront their own social status.

In Namibia these statements of first principle take on a special significance, for in Namibia, as in South Africa, a person's race determines his or her chances of enjoying good health. The practice of apartheid in Namibia is the most immediate and abhorrent feature that strikes a sensitive visitor new to the region. Such blatant discrimination motivates most Christian and liberal consciences to action, so that fighting apartheid can draw on wide support. But there is a danger when we focus on the immediate and obvious disadvantages suffered by one race and inflicted by another, a danger that we will fight only on that front and lose sight of the underlying inequalities being inflicted by one class upon another.

Racial divisions are part of a colonial system that maintained its legitimacy through arguments of racial, cultural and spiritual superiority. In fact the colonisers' strength lay in technology, particularly guns, but also farming and mining techniques. White superiority served well to justify the pioneers' barbarism, to inspire their troops and to intimidate the colonised. But behind the racial justifications lay the real relationships of class – of ownership and control of the means of producing wealth (including health). The abolition of racial discrimination will not in itself destroy the class structure. All too easily a well established class system can absorb such shocks without excessive damage, just as it has absorbed the abolition of slavery, the abolition of religious discrimination, and may yet absorb the abolition of sexual discrimination.

Of course racist ideology must be confronted. Fighting apartheid in the name of human rights can and does motivate a large number of people. The greatest value, however, lies in the consciousness-raising use of these campaigns – asking the questions: *How is it that one person is in a position to discriminate against another in the first place? How can it be prevented?*

These questions form the background to this book, and the various chapters try in different ways to look at the politics of practicing health and health care. Coming as the book does, however, from a series of papers and workshops given at an international conference,[1] with discussions and further material contributed during and after the conference, it is inevitable that the book will vary quite a lot in style, in the depth of its analysis, and the degree to which the politics of health are explicitly considered.

Given the various sources that have contributed to this book, it follows that the book does not reflect the views of the Namibia Support Committee.

Nor indeed does it reflect those of SWAPO. The views, comments, ideas and suggestions that the book contains are published as a resource since the wealth of material arising at the conference deserves a proper record and a wider audience.

The chapters following this introduction set the general scene. Chapter 2 looks at the situation in Namibia under South African occupation, providing a summary of the health statistics of the population and an overview of the health service structure which is likely to be inherited at independence. Chapter 3 then examines the role of women, their status in Namibia and their relation to the production of good health in the family as well as their predominance in the nursing services.

Chapter 4 then takes a broad look at the causes of ill-health in underdeveloped countries. It shows ill-health to be embedded in poverty, itself a product of colonial relations. Medical solutions are largely irrelevant. The emphasis is on the ability of communities to organise themselves, and relate to the formal health services through Community Health Workers, elected by and answerable to their community.

Chapter 5 considers the orientation of health workers, looking first at a range of other countries' experiences organising their health services after independence, and then asking what conclusions may be drawn about the nature of the services and the role of the professional health worker in them. Health workers' training is examined, including their political orientation and their relationship to the people they serve.

This is followed by a series of discussions of what a re-organised health service may need to consider, both the general principles involved in establishing primary care and preventive programmes, and specific experiences of such programmes in underdeveloped countries including Mozambique and Zimbabwe.

Chapter 7 concerns the health of urban residents and industrial workers, and the services available to them. These are discussed in the context of the needs of industrial management to have a healthy labour force – at least a healthy skilled labour force – as well as provide themselves with the best facilities available in western medicine. The chapter also considers how the activities of multinationals, including their exploitation of the uranium resources, affects the health of the population.

A further chapter follows, looking at medical and pharmaceutical supplies for the health services, and suggesting some areas where an incoming Namibian government might wish to focus attention. Chapter 9 then takes us back where this introduction began, with the telling of a simple story. It is one of a range of methods described for both health workers and community groups to use, in order to learn for themselves about the politics of health.

There is then a short concluding chapter expressing our support for the continuing struggle to bring health to the people of Namibia. An Appendix follows, giving the names and addresses of some organisations able to provide further information, followed by a list of publications on Namibia, health and underdevelopment.

## References

1  *International Seminar on Health in Namibia*, held at the City University, London, October 1983.

# Health in contemporary Namibia

The picture of health in Namibia is a divided one. There are two Namibias and two nations. The first, the world of white Namibians, is a world of comfort and plenty, of good health and high quality facilities for the sick. The Namibians of the first world live long, comparatively pleasant lives and when they die it is usually from the 'diseases of affluent living' or from old age.

The second world, the world of most black Namibians, is a harsh, uncomfortable one in which life is a scramble for the resources needed to survive. For most, it is a world of illness, hunger and deprivation. Treatment of the ill is brusque, and in poor conditions, with a low chance of recovery. The Namibians of this second world live shorter lives and die from the diseases of poverty, overwork and poor nutrition.

The physical world of Namibia is also a divided one: divided between rural and urban, and between the north and the south. Namibia is a large country, about four times the size of Britain, with a population of one and a quarter million people. The climate is harsh, temperature variations are extreme and the already inadequate rainfall is exacerbated by frequent drought. The climate in the north of the country favours tropical diseases such as malaria and bilharzia. The dry climate in the south encourages respiratory diseases such as bronchitis and tuberculosis.

Living conditions in rural areas are poor. Much of the better farming land is reserved for white-owned commercial farming so that despite the relatively low overall population density, fertile land is scarce for most Namibians. They are crowded into the 'reserved' areas, where the land is overworked and of poor quality. The contract labour system has forced a high proportion of the able-bodied men to migrate in search of jobs, with the result that the burdens of childcare and agricultural production fall largely on women. There are too few boreholes and wells to supplement the surface water and provide plentiful and secure water supplies. Proper sanitation facilities are virtually non-existent in most areas.

In urban areas most black Namibians are overcrowded, and some lack electricity or running water. Incomes are low for most black workers and general levels of nutrition are poor. Living in these conditions results in a high incidence of contagious and infectious diseases. In addition, workers in mines, factories and on the commercial farms are subjected to dangerous and exhausting conditions contributing to accidents and occupational diseases.

## A.   The Political System in Occupied Namibia

Health conditions in Namibia and the determinants of health and illness cannot be properly understood without some knowledge of the political system prevailing in that country. For a hundred years Namibians have been ruled by foreigners and for a hundred years they have struggled against foreign occupation and have been hunted down, shot, hanged, starved and imprisoned. Despite this oppression, the struggle for freedom has continued. For nearly twenty years the People's Liberation Army of Namibia (PLAN, the armed wing of SWAPO of Namibia – the national liberation movement) has taken up arms against the current military occupation of the country by South African forces. South Africa has been the *de facto* ruler of the country since 1915 and, despite International Court rulings that its presence in Namibia is llegal and that the legal administrative body is the United Nations, South Africa has refused to withdraw its troops and officials.

Not only does South Africa continue to occupy Namibia illegally and despite resolutions in the United Nations General Assembly and the Security Council, but it has introduced its apartheid system into the country – a system of legalised racism, in which racial discrimination is written into the country's constitution. Since 1981 South Africa has imposed on Namibia a three-tier government structure. The top tier is a single body run by South African officials who control nationally-based services including the general economy, the police services and the armed forces. The second teir is composed of 11 'ethnic' authorities, one for each of the categories into which the South Africans have divided the black population plus one for whites. Each ethnic authority is responsible for major social services such as education, health and local administration serving the 11 groups defined under the apartheid categories. The third tier is that of municipal government of the principal towns and is dominated by whites. They have retained control of a supposedly non-racial level of government by demanding qualifications and gerrymandering electorates to exclude black Namibians. The result of this system of government is gross inequalities in state spending and allocation of resources.

# B.   Inequality of state provision

Each year the central government pays amounts calculated on a per capita basis to the ethnic administrations to provide the services under their control. The ethnic administrations are expected to raise further resources, however, through taxation of their 'own group'. The result is a continuation and even a worsening of the inequalities. All money raised from the wealthy white population is spent on white services. Where black populations are too poor for further taxation to be feasible no additional revenues are raised and no further money is available to spend on their services. In 1982/3 the central allocation to the White Administration was R12 million. Total spending by the White Administration was R114.7 million! For education alone, the White Administration spent some R1,762 per pupil. Table 1 gives comparable figures for some of the other ethnic administrations.

*Table 1:   Spending on Education by Ethnic Administrations*[1]

| Ethnic Authority | Total Spending per Pupil |
| --- | --- |
| Baster | R368 |
| Damara | R324 |
| Coloured | R673 |
| Nama | R398 |
| Tswana | R465 |
| White | R1,762 |

Even these figures disguise the extent of the inequalities, however, for many Namibians receive no schooling whatsoever. In 1980 under 40% of Namibians received some form of primary education, and only ten percent of these went on to receive secondary education. Education to the age of 16 is compulsory for all white children with the result that most finish with some secondary qualifications and many go on to tertiary level. In contrast only one percent of blacks have secondary qualifications while 64% have little or no formal education.[2]

In the health services similar inequalities prevail. Facilities are segregated on the basis of the 11 apartheid categories. In 1980/1 health spending for whites was R233.70 per person compared with spending for blacks ranging from R4.70 to R56.84 per person. The emphasis of the health services is on curative rather than preventive care, with high technology provided for the white population. Such preventive programmes that did exist have been severely disrupted by the war, leading to increases in malaria, tuberculosis, typhoid, bubonic plague and other preventable diseases.

## C.   Unequal access to resources

There are estimated to be one and a quarter million Namibians, and although the average population density in Namibia is under four people per square mile, the distribution is in fact very uneven, with some areas virtually uninhabited and others overcrowded. Half the land is occupied by white commercial farms, although whites constitute barely seven per cent of the population. Of the ranching land, 80% is owned by some 5,000 white cattle owners while 20,000 black families raise their cattle on the remainder. The majority of all black farmers, 120,000 Namibian families, live in the north of the country on just five per cent of the viable farmland.

Much of Namibia is desert or semi-desert country unsuitable for rain-dependent cultivation. Apart from the northern areas, most water has to be brought to the surface from deep boreholes or wells or captured and pumped through irrigation schemes. Most of these artificial water sources have been constructed to benefit the white population. Even where there is usually sufficient surface water, intermittent drought makes supplies unreliable. Black Namibians, who rely on the natural surface water once again suffer disproportionately during periods of low rainfall.

Namibia is a relatively wealthy country rich in minerals and precious stones. Gross Domestic Product in 1980 was R1,323 million, which is an average of R1,200 per person. The country has been one of the world's largest exporters of gem diamonds since 1908, is a major uranium producer (the uranium is being illegally extracted by Rio Tinto Zinc Corporation) and has large reserves of other metals. Mineral extraction accounts for nearly half of Namibia's wealth (46.5% of GDP). But the majority of Namibians are very poor. Some 12% of the GDP finds its way to the black population, although they constitute over 90% of the population. 56% of GDP goes to company profits, and a massive 33% of GDP flows out of the country every year.[3]

## D.   Mortality

The disparities in the standards of living and in the access to resources are reflected in the mortality rates for the different populations in Namibia. No national statistics for mortality in Namibia exist because there is no legal requirement for the registration of births and deaths. Figures are available for Windhoek, the largest city, however. Death rates for Whites are 7.4 per thousand people, for Coloureds 12.4 per 1,000 and for Africans 17.1 per 1,000. These figures for Windhoek do not represent the national situation because there are large numbers of single men living in the single-sex hostels in Katutura, an African suburb of Windhoek. The disparities in infant mortality rates are more stark: among Windhoek Whites the rates are 21.6 per 1,000 live births, among Coloureds 145 per 1,000 and among Africans 165 per 1,000. The average life expectancy of a black person in Namibia is 40 years compared with a 70 year average in Europe.[4]

# E. Disease

Official, but inadequate, figures show that gastro-enteritis (diarrhoea) is by far the most common illness among infants, and tuberculosis the most common among adults. Urban black Namibians also show high rates of cancer, hypertension and stroke, with heart disease particularly prominent among Coloureds. Measles, osteo-arthritis, bronchitis, pneumonia, whooping cough and impetigo are also prevalent.[5]

Social conditions in Windhoek's black townships have contributed to high levels of alcoholism affecting nearly half the population. Stress also contributes to the 'huge quantities' of tranquilizers consumed, especially by mineworkers.[6]

Venereal disease is common among both urban and rural populations. Almost 10% of the adult population of Kavango was found to be affected, 4% of the coastal town of Swakopmund, and 5% of black adults in Windhoek. The situation is deteriorating and is being blamed on the lack of curative and preventive services. One doctor estimated that over 95% of all adult black males in Namibia would contract venereal disease in their lifetimes.[7]

Cancer levels are unusually high for an underdeveloped country. One out of six adult deaths is a result of cancer and levels in Namibia are over twice those in South Africa. Among women, cervical cancer is particularly common. Both the widespread use of unsealed asbestos in the houses built by the state for black Namibians, and the effects of uranium mining on mineworkers, their families and nearby residents, have been cited as contributory causes to the high cancer levels.[8]

Malaria is endemic in the north of Namibia and periodically becomes epidemic. The intensification of South Africa's war against SWAPO and PLAN has disrupted mosquito control programmes. In 1982 malaria was at its highest level in 20 years. By that year only a fifth of the northern part of Namibia was still being sprayed against mosquitos. In 1982 many health institutions ran out of medicine to treat malaria. By February 1984 doctors at Oshakati Hospital said they were admitting ten cases of cerebral malaria every week and simply dosing and discharging non-cerebral cases due to a shortage of space.[9]

Another endemic disease, bubonic plague, reached epidemic proportions in 1983. 548 cases were confirmed and 14 people were known to have died of the disease between March 1983 and February 1984. Many others are thought to have died in remote rural areas not served by curative services. The numbers of cases may also be swollen by the tens of thousands of people fleeing the war or being contained in 'squatter camps' in the north of Namibia. South African troops in the area were protected by a 5 ton shipment of rat poison flown in by the authorities and being spread around the perimeters of the fortified military camps.[10]

A German Development Institute study in 1980 found a high incidence of tuberculosis. In some areas 25% of the population was found to be suffering from the disease. T.B. is associated with poor living conditions and general poverty, and a Windhoek doctor has estimated that the incidence among the black population is thirty times higher than that among the white population. Hepatitis, diphtheria, parasitic diseases and rabies are also common in Namibia.[11]

# G.   The Health System

The burden of preventable disease falls on those who neither own nor control significant means of production – the peasants and workers. About ¾ of the population live in the reserved 'homelands' or 'Bantustans' to which they are relegated by apartheid laws. Less than one in five doctors in Namibia work in these areas, and only a fifth of the nation's health budget is spent there. Greatest spending is on the prestigious hospitals in the urban areas, institutions which do not contribute to the maintenance of health but are devoted to the treatment of ill-health. As Dr Indongo, SWAPO Secretary for Health and Social Welfare, has said, the system is far from being oriented towards primary health care but is 'urban biased and orientated towards curative medicine'.[12]

Attempts to run 10 different health services in Namibia, one for each apartheid category (the service for the San ethnic group is subsumed into that for whites) has resulted in chaos, corruption and inefficiency. By 1984 all but three of the services were in fact being run by the wealthy white administration on an agency basis, and of the remaining three the Ovambo service was being run by the military on the pretext of saving it from collapse.

The figures for spending on education showed great discrepancies and the same is found in health care. Figures for 1981 show expenditure per person on health as follows:

Table 2:   Per Capita Spending on Health Services[13]

| Ethnic Authority | Total Spending per Person |
| --- | --- |
| Rehoboth (Baster) | R4.70 |
| Damara | R15.02 |
| Ovambo | R24.85 |
| Caprivi | R37.06 |
| Kavango | R56.84 |
| Whites | R233.70 |

One of the effects of the division of the health service is the exacerbation of already serious staff shortages and service deficiencies. There are serious shortages of all types of medical, nursing and other trained staff which, with the lack of repair and maintenance of facilities, has led to increasing numbers of patients being refused treatment. The adverse effects of the fragmentation of the health service has been so marked that the Broeksma Commission of inquiry into health provision appointed by the South Africans found almost unanimous opposition to the system among health personnel. The Commission found that out of 10 ethnic administrations only that of whites was in favour of retaining the present system, and the Commission recommended a return to a unitary service.

# H.  Corruption

Another effect of the fragmentation of the service has been an increase in corruption among those politicians who have chosen to collaborate with the South African apartheid system. A second Commission set up to investigate corruption in government services in Namibia found evidence that it was widespread in the health services. The Thirion Commission heard of the delivery of inferior quality and overpriced equipment to hospitals in exchange for bribes to officials. Gifts and favours were provided by South African companies in exchange for contracts for drugs and medical supplies. Evidence was given of illicit payments made to the Chief Radiographer of Windhoek State Hospital, and a 'consultancy fee' of R20,000 paid to an employee of the Department of Hospital Services. One state pharmacist even sold government medicines to state hospitals for his own profit.[14]

While the Thirion hearings were proceeding, two leading doctors were being charged with defrauding the state of R173,000 through submitting false claims for the use of private aircraft to transport patients.[15]

# I.  Non-State Health Services

The health services in Namibia could not function without the contribution of churches and missions. Most of the small rural hospitals and clinics are run by church organisations and subsidised to varying extents by the state. The sympathy of some mission staff for the political aspirations of the Namibian people, and declarations that they will treat all those in need – including PLAN soldiers – has led to restrictions on the numbers of foreign medical staff being allowed into the country by South Africa, and attempts to intimidate foreign and local people working in the non-state sector. The resulting staff shortfall has been partly made up by military personnel seconded from the South African forces to the hospitals, thereby further increasing South African control of the health services.

Some clinics and two small hospitals are provided by mining companies operating in Namibia. Access to these facilities is usually limited to the mineworkers employed by the companies.

# J.  Health Personnel and Facilities

In 1973 there were 74 hospitals and 54 clinics in Namibia providing an average of eight beds per thousand people. By 1982 this had declined to 56 hospitals and 50 clinics with a corresponding drop in beds available. In 1979 there were 126 general practitioners and 26 specialist doctors, 16 dentists, and 665 qualified and 140 enrolled nurses. No training facilities for doctors exist in Namibia.

Such aggregate figures are the only ones released by the South African authorities and give a distorted picture of the true situation. According to official sources we may calculate, for example, that with 152 doctors in Namibia the ratio is one doctor for every 6,600 people. But with only 20% of doctors practising in the rural areas where 75% of Namibians live, the real ratio in those areas is nearer one doctor for every 26,000 people, and some estimates of the real rural population would put the figure at one doctor for some 35,000 people. Of the 16 dentists in Namibia, none at all are based in the rural areas. Hospital bed provision is also difficult to interpret – the official rate is one bed per 130 people, but the term 'bed' includes the floor mats provided to many blacks in their overcrowded facilities so the bed numbers are very flexible and the corresponding use of services is not easy to establish.

## K.  Other Social Services

State compensation provisions for injuries at work exclude out-workers and domestic workers (almost all black) and discriminate in payments according to white and black wage levels. State pensions are similarly discriminatory, with white pensioners receiving three times as much as black pensioners.

There are no rehabilitation centres for alcoholics in Namibia, but White and Coloured patients may be referred to clinics in South Africa. Despite an estimated 50,000 disabled people, many of them war victims, only 2,000 people were receiving institutional assistance in 1981. State provisions for childcare and recreation for black children appear to be non-existent, the only services being provided by the churches or other voluntary organisations. The only orphanage in Namibia is restricted to white children and in 1983 only 80 of its 140 places were filled.

There are no institutions for elderly black people. When residents of Epako, the black suburb of Gobabis, requested an old-aged home, the white Town Clerk replied:

> 'It is the first time I hear the request for an old-aged home. Even if they had done so in the past, I doubt whether we would have built one because nowhere in South West Africa is there an old-aged home for blacks.'[16]

## L.  The Impact of the War

Like other areas of life in Namibia, the South African regime produces no statistics on the impact of the war on the people of the country. Unlike other areas, it has also made it an offence to give any information on the war unless previously authorised by the government. Any picture of the impact of the war is, therefore, necessarily impressionistic and patchy. Despite this, however, it is clear that its effects have touched on every family in Namibia.

In 1983 the war was costing South Africa some R2 million every day. There are some 100,000 South African-controlled troops deployed in Namibia, mostly in the north where the ratio is about one for every five civilians. Despite one of the heaviest concentrations of forces in the world, PLAN continues to operate in the area and SWAPO enjoys widespread support among the people. Since the start of fighting over 10,000 Namibians – one percent of the population – have died in the war. Many more have been injured and almost 10 percent of the population have fled the country.

Since 1978 there has been a marked change in tactics by the South Africans who have shifted the burden of the fighting onto black Namibians to reduce the disquiet growing among white conscripts. Most notorious of the forces set up to achieve this is 'Koevoet' (or Crowbar), a special police unit now responsible for over 80% of war deaths in Ovambo and Kavango. Koevoet members are paid bounties of R2,000 for each PLAN soldier killed, R1,000 for an AK47 rifle captured and R5,000 for a SAM 7 missile. No investigations are undertaken to substantiate Koevoet claims that those killed are indeed PLAN members. Effectively, all able-bodied Namibians have a R2,000 price on their heads.

Torture of detainees is routine for Koevoet, and arbitrary killings have at times become so crude that members of the unit have been prosecuted. Generally, though, they are left alone.

Apart from those physically maimed by the war, the trauma and brutality experienced by many people has resulted in a high incidence of mental illness and psychosis. Even the Namibian Attorney General acknowledged in 1983 that the effect of the war had been to make life cheap. Assault has become common and theft widespread, and over a third of all criminal cases brought before the courts involve members of the official armed forces.

Not only has the war increased the numbers requiring medical treatment, disrupted food production, education and community life generally, but it has also seriously damaged such health services as had existed, especially in the north. The incidence of plague, malaria, typhoid, tuberculosis and venereal disease have been boosted to epidemic levels by the war. The military curfew has prevented people travelling at night however serious their medical needs may be, and hospitals have been bombed, burnt down or simply closed by the South African forces.

In addition, more and more hospitals in the 'war zone' have been taken over by the military. In 1983 a Chief of Staff in the SWA Territory Force announced that of 58 doctors in Kaokoland 49 were soldiers, and all dentists, psychologists and veterinary surgeons in the area were military personnel.

## M.   Conclusion

Many of the diseases now rife in Namibia were unknown in the area a hundred years ago. They were introduced by Europeans and spread rapidly among a defenceless local population. During the century of occupation Namibians have experienced a decline in their standard of diet. They have had much of their good agricultual land taken from them. They have been forced into a cash economy with its concomitant migrant labour system leading to the disruption of family groupings and communal support networks.

Poverty and disease have increased and now, with the military occupation, Namibians are experiencing possibly the worst levels of ill-health in their history. The means of preventing ill-health have been taken from them and in their place are a few meagre and discriminatory curative services. An independent Namibia will inherit this legacy of colonialism and will be left to mend the damage that colonial underdevelopment created.

## References

1 *Namibian Review* No 25, July-Aug 1982, pp 15-16.
2 *Windhoek Observer* 19.3.83.
3 *South African Occupation and the Namibian Economy* Catholic Institute for International Relations, London, 1984.
4 *Windhoek Advertiser* 5.5.81 & 3.9.83; D. Simon 'The Crisis in Namibian Health Services', *Namibian Review* April-June 1983, p 16.
5 D. Simon *op. cit.*
6 D. Simon *op. cit.*; *Windhoek Advertiser* 4.4.81, 5.5.81, 7.8.81, 20.11.81 & 30.6.83.
7 *Windhoek Advertiser* 1.8.80, 5.5.81 & 4.2.83.
8 *Windhoek Observer* 18.11.81; M. Murphy 'Working on the Nuclear Chain Gang' *Action on Namibia* No 2, 1983, p 13.
9 *Windhoek Advertiser* 9.6.82 & 5.11.82; *Cape Times* 17.2.84.
10 A. Weaver 'Caught in the Crossfire: The War in Namibia', *Work in Progress* No 29, Oct 1983, p 8.
11 *Windhoek Advertiser* 1.8.80, 5.8.81 & 14.8.81; *Rand Daily Mail* 14.3.83.
12 Quoted in *Action in Namibia* No 2, 1983, special issue on health, p 1.
13 *Windhoek Advertiser* 18.11.81; D. Simon *op. cit.*
14 *Windhoek Advertiser* 19.7.83 & 1.8.83; *Briefing on the Situation in Namibia*, International Defence and Aid Fund, London, 27.10.83, p 9.
15 *Windhoek Advertiser* 18.11.83.
16 *Windhoek Advertiser* 25.5.83.

See also: *Children of Namibia: Growing Up Under Apartheid* IDAF Briefing Paper No. 10, March 1984; and A. Seedat *Crippling a Nation: Health in Apartheid South Africa*, IDAF, April 1984.

**Black poverty**

**White affluance**

# 3
# Namibian women: battling for survival

Women constitute a large proportion of the rural population in Namibia, and primary health care strategies can have a major impact on their lives. Women are also in the majority in the health professions, mostly in the nursing and caring services.[1] Over 2,000 women work in the nursing services, most of them as unqualified assistants and aides.

Thus in both the formal health services and in the day-to-day living of families, it is women who maintain the health of much of the national population, especially away from the urban centres. This chapter looks at the conditions under which women perform this role and how it is related to the forms of ill-health that women themselves suffer.

## In the Bantustans

The majority of black women live in the 'homelands' – barren dumping grounds from which the men migrate in search of work in the mines and industries. For long periods of their lives, women in these bantustans are the sole providers, doing backbreaking agricultural work, bringing up their children, taking care of the aged. There are few paid jobs in the bantustans. Women rely on whatever they can produce and on remittances from their husbands. Their harsh lives in the bantustans inevitably affect their health.

Mathilda Nanyemba, a leading member of SWAPO, described their plight:

'After spending up to seven hours of backbreaking labour in the fields, women in the rural areas do not return to rest for the day. They must fetch water, grind grain into flour, prepare meals, not to mention washing the babies and their diapers ... There is a severe shortage of clinics and hospitals in the rural areas. Malaria is always endemic in these areas, especially during the wet, rainy seasons. Although the rainy season is when people should spend much time cultivating their fields, more often than not you find women flocking with their children on their backs to far distant clinics in search of scarce medical services.'[2]

**Women's work – hoeing**

In the north of the country, which has been under a state of emergency for over ten years, there are additional hazards in seeking medical treatment. A night curfew prevents people from travelling after dark, and medical teams have stopped going to certain areas where the war is particularly intense. The few hospitals, mostly run by the churches, are greatly overcrowded. Journalists visiting one mission hospital in the Ovambo region in October 1982 found that the maternity ward, with 35 beds, was accommodating 78 patients. The mothers could only stay on for a minimum period after the birth to make way for new patients. Most had arrived days or weeks before their confinement, staying at nearby quarters which were described as 'unhygienic'. They have been forced to make a long journey which, if left too late, would have been even more hazardous in an emergency.[3]

Harsh living conditions, poverty, malnutrition and the lack of medical services combine to make women in the rural areas greatly vulnerable to the many endemic diseases which, through a lack of immunisation programmes and unhygienic conditions, continue to be common in Namibia.

## Urban Stress

Only about 73,000 out of a total of some 240,000 black wage earners are women. The majority, about 60,000, work as domestic servants in white households, the lowest paid category of wage earners. In the black townships they have to fend for themselves and their children on an average income for domestic work of R20 to R40 a month.[4] This is too little to pay for food, housing, clothing and other basic necessities. The acute shortage of housing means several families have to occupy one small house. One survey in 1983 found up to 35 people living in a two-bedroomed house.[5] Many women have no home at all, staying 'illegally' in the men's quarters, where contract workers are housed as 'single men' whether they are married or not.

The result of these conditions is a level of deprivation and poverty which imposes enormous stress, affecting both womens' physical and mental health. A social worker in Katutura, the black township outside Windhoek, described the effect these conditions have on women. She noted in many women a sense of rootlessness and insecurity, a constant shifting from place to place, often accompanied by two or three children. 'Children are hungry, they want clothes, but she's got no money. She thinks and thinks and worries about this all the time, until she becomes mentally unbalanced'.

The social worker found many health-related complaints such as heart palpitations, headaches, lameness, loss of speech, anxiety, faintness and hypertension.[6]

Resistance to illness is weakened by poor diet, consisting mainly of mealie meal and bread, with occasional vegetables. Frieda Williams, an executive member of SWAPO Women's Council, pointed out that people's diet in the urban areas was influenced by Western concepts imposed by the South African illegal presence, and by the lack of facilities to grow their own food. While the traditional diet was meat, milk and mealie or maize porridge, they were now influenced to prefer rice or macaroni. Similarly, young mothers were turning away from breastfeeding towards bottlefeeding because of the advertising from multinational companies, and because it was extremely difficult to hold down a job while breastfeeding. Infants had to be weaned at three months and sent back to relatives in the bantustans so that women could go back to work. Employers could also just sack a woman who got pregnant.[7]

As domestic servants, black women suffer low pay, long hours of work, and constant anxiety about their own children, left behind to fend for themselves. One Namibian domestic worker described her experience:

'We as housewives must leave our children at home during the day, because there are no centres to look after our children. When we come home after work we find our houses dirty, we have to clean the children now without care – they have stayed hungry the whole day . . . most of the time the children go to the dirt-bins to scratch for food.'[8]

There appear to be no facilities to help women make an informed choice about having children. Family planning in the context of apartheid can be used as a means to keep down the black population, and black women are clearly aware of this. Frieda Williams, who worked as a nurse in Namibia during the early 1970s, found that black mothers were being injected with Depo Provera after the delivery of their babies, without their knowledge. Depo Provera has been banned or restricted in many countries because it can produce irregular bleeding and nausea and possibly even more dangerous side-effects. In some cases the woman had her uterus removed after Caesarian section, again without her consent.[9]

## Women in the Refugee Camps

In the SWAPO-run Health and Education Centres – the refugee settlements of Kwanza Sul in Angola and Nayango in Zambia – the majority of the 80-100,000 refugees are women and children. SWAPO has already implemented a health programme which provides basic services and emphasises training and community oriented health care. Pregnant women

**Women's work – carrying water**

are looked after by other women, and mothers are trained in basic preventive health care. A record system monitors the development of young children, kept up to date by the mothers themselves. A survey of women found as many as 99% to be illiterate, and SWAPO Women's Council is introducing a literacy training programme using health education material.

Many of those arriving at the Centres bring disease including typhoid, malaria, gastro-enteritis and parasitic infections. Some are also suffering from tuberculosis. Day-care facilities are being provided, as are rehabilitation programmes for the war-wounded and disabled, and a training programme for medical students, nurses and midwives.

Many refugees arrive in states of psychological shock and trauma, and SWAPO's political education work is one of the main safeguards against the development of mental illnesses. It is used to explain and help people to understand the events they have experienced prior to their arrival at the Centre.

Women play a major role in developing agricultural projects with the aim of becoming self-sufficient in fresh foods, whilst at the same time learning about the causes and solutions to malnourishment among their children.

With the serious shortages and hardships, SWAPO has appealed to the international community for medical supplies and clothing, and for maternity and childcare material aid, including soaps and creams, sanitary towels and baby clothes.


## Health as a Right

Until South Africa's illegal occupation of Namibia is ended, there is not likely to be much improvement in the conditions under which black women – and all black people – live, and which are the main causes of ill-health. Apartheid treats black women as 'superfluous appendages' whose health is of little importance.

SWAPO's health policy stresses the importance of women's health by providing health education, maternal and child health care, and basic literacy training which enables women to learn about the nutritional, hygiene and other aspects of primary health care which will form the basis of health provision in an independent Namibia. In the refugee settlements in Angola and Zambia, Namibian women are experiencing for the first time a concern for their well-being.


## References

1  SWAPO of Namibia, *To Be Born a Nation: The Liberation Struggle for Namibia*, Zed Press, London 1981, p 328.
2  *Namibian Women's Struggle and Solidarity in Britain*, SWAPO Women's Council and SWAPO Women's Solidarity Campaign, May 1981.
3  *Windhoek Advertiser* 26.10.82.
4  *Windhoek Observer* 6.3.82; *Windhoek Advertiser* 30.6.83.
5  *The Namibian Review* No. 27, Jan-March 1983; No. 28, April-June 1983.
6  *Windhoek Advertiser* 30.6.83.
7  *Anti-Apartheid News*, November 1982.
8  *Namibian Women's Struggle, op. cit.*
9  *Anti-Apartheid News, op. cit.*

# The struggle for health

This chapter deals with health and health care in underdeveloped countries in general and in the Southern African region in particular. It shows how the politics and economics of racial oppression and economic underdevelopment are associated with both an unacceptable disease burden and an inappropriate health service. Any quest for improved health and more appropriate and accessible health care requires a successful struggle both *against* colonial underdevelopment and *for* fundamental changes in the political economy, and within this, the health sector itself.

First it looks at health problems in colonial and post-colonial countries and locates them within their social, political and economic context. It looks critically at how these health problems have been approached in the past and suggests how an approach to health and health care could be developed which might strengthen democracy and collective self-reliance, both crucial ingredients in the struggle for liberation and health.

## Health and Disease in Society

### A.   Mortality and Morbidity

Reliable information on the amount and effects of different diseases is not available for many underdeveloped countries. This is the case for the majority population groups in Southern Africa and is itself an indication of the poor infrastructure and services for the mass of the people.

Infant and early childhood mortality (death) rates are especially pertinent in underdeveloped countries where typically half the population is under 15 years old and 20% under the age of 5, and where young childhood deaths may account for a third or even a half of all deaths. Women in their fertile period contribute another 20% of such countries' populations, and together with the under-5s comprise some 40%. This combined vulnerable group probably accounts for two-thirds of the major health problems. That the situation in Namibia is almost certainly like this general pattern is shown by the infant mortality rates for the major city, Windhoek, where the rates between 1970 and 1975 were 163 deaths per 1,000 black infants, 145 per 1,000 'coloured' infants and 21 per 1,000 white infants.[1] The rate is likely to be even higher for rural blacks, with perhaps over 200 per 1,000 liveborn infants dying in their first year of life.[2]

## B.  Disease Patterns

The major causes of disease and death in children are depressingly similar in different underdeveloped countries and bear a striking resemblance to the diseases prevalent in the industrialised countries less than a century ago (see Table 1).

Table 1:   Causes of Death in Infants and Children Under Five Years Old – %.[3]

| | London 1903 | Matlab Bangladesh 1975/7 | Haiti 1979/ 1980 | Java 1979 | Narangwal India 1971/73 |
|---|---|---|---|---|---|
| Diarrhoea and Enteritis | 13 | 29 | 15 | 15 | 39 |
| Pneumonia and other Respiratory | 17 | 6 | 12 | 21 | 19 |
| Malnutrition incl. low birth weight | 26 | – | 33 | 22 | 5 |
| Immunizable Diseases: | | | | | |
| Tetanus | 4 | 14 | 3 | 8 | 2 |
| Whooping Cough | 4 | – | 1 | – | – |
| Measles | 3 | 8 | 1 | 6 | 1 |
| Tuberculosis | 4 | – | 3 | – | – |
| Others | 29 | 57 | 31 | 28 | 34 |
| Death Rate per 1,000 | 145 | 280 | 200 | 100 | 135 |
| Age groups | (0-1) | (0-4) | (0-4) | (0-2) | (0-3) |

For underdeveloped countries' populations in general the most common diseases and causes of death fall into two main groups – nutritional deficiencies and communicable diseases – and can be classified according to Table 2.

These categories – nutritional and communicable – interact with and aggravate each other. Undernutrition, especially of children, is a crucial factor as it makes the individual vulnerable to the most important infectious diseases causing death – diarrhoea, measles and tuberculosis. Although no reliable figures are available for Namibia, 'nutritional deficiencies probably

Table 2: The Classification of Most Diseases in Underdeveloped Countries.[4]

| NUTRITIONAL | Airborne | COMMUNICABLE |
|---|---|---|
| | | Water-related, vector-borne and faecally-transmitted |
| *Undernutrition* and associated vitamin deficiencies | *1. Viral*<br>Influenza<br>Pneumonia<br>Measles<br>Chickenpox<br>Smallpox* | *1. Water-borne or water-related*<br>Cholera<br>Typhoid<br>Diarrhoea, dysenteries and amoebiasis<br>Infectious hepatitis, poliomyelitis and intestinal worms |
| | *2. Bacterial*<br>Whooping cough<br>Diphtheria<br>Meningitis<br>Tuberculosis | *2. Water-washed*<br>(a) Skin and eye infections<br>Trachoma<br>Skin infection<br>(b) Skin infestation<br>Leprosy<br>Scabies<br>Louse-borne typhus* |
| | | *3. Water-based*<br>(a) Penetrating skin<br>Bilharzia (schistosomiasis)<br>(b) Ingested<br>Guinea worm* |
| | | *4. Water-related insect vectors*<br>(a) Biting near water<br>Sleeping sickness*<br>(b) Breeding near water<br>Malaria<br>River blindness (onchocersiasis)* |

* Not found in Namibia

NOTES
*Airborne:* spread by breathing airborne, respiratory secretions from an infected person;
*Water-borne:* spread when the pathogen is in the water drunk by people who may then get infected;
*Water-washed:* spread by the hands, cooking utensils etc, but the chance of catching the disease falls when more water for drinking and hygiene is used (whatever the quality of the water);
*Water-based:* the pathogen spends part of its life-cycle in an aquatic animal (e.g. a snail).

constitute a major health problem.'[5] Maternal undernutrition gives rise to serious health problems by contributing to difficult labour and newborn birth injury, and to low birth weight babies who are more susceptible to fatal conditions in the early period of life.

The airborne diseases most commonly causing death in Southern Africa are pneumonia, measles and tuberculosis. Measles is much more serious in the undernourished child and blindness is frequently a sequel in those with dietary vitamin A deficiency. The incidence and severity of pneumonia probably relates more to overcrowded living conditions than undernutrition. Tuberculosis, too, is worse where living conditions are poor, and is also related to bad working conditions (particularly atmospheric) as well as low levels of nutrition.

Of the faecally-transmitted and water-related diseases, enteric and diarrhoeal diseases are the most important, particularly among young undernourished children. Any significant reduction in these depends on both better nutrition and greater quantities of clean (but not necessarily pure) water.

Other 'water-washed' diseases include intestinal worms, trachoma–a major cause of blindness in arid areas – and scabies. The severity of many of these diseases can be related to nutritional status. The two important vector-borne diseases of malaria and schistosomiasis (bilharzia) are both water-related.

Mental ill-health previously regarded as uncommon in underdeveloped countries has now been shown to occur as frequently in these situations as in industrialised countries. This is hardly surprising given the stresses on people living under oppression and deprivation. The number of people suffering mental illnesses – and the number suffering many physical illnesses – increases greatly at times of conflict, such as that presently occurring in Namibia, among both residents and refugees.

In summary, the diseases most frequently suffered by the majority of the population of Southern Africa consist mainly of nutritional deficiencies and communicable diseases, the two types acting synergistically. The pattern is typical of underdeveloped countries. The diseases arise from the conditions of poverty with its associated problems of inadequate nutrition, poor water supply, unsanitary and overcrowded living conditions and dangerous and dirty working environments. Furthermore, the poor social conditions giving rise to this disease pattern are aggravated by the continuing conflict in the region.

By contrast, the disease burden of the small, mostly white minority consists mainly of degenerative vascular conditions and cancer. They, too, are traceable to living and working conditions, although these are substantially different from those experienced by the vast majority of the population.

## C.  Interventions Needed to Promote Health

The single most important action needed to promote the health of the majority of people is to improve *nutrition*. This is discussed in greater depth in Chapter 6, Part 4, but a few points need to be made here.

Recent research has shown that undernutrition syndromes previously attributed to protein deficiency are in fact due to general food and energy deficiency. If a person does not take in enough calories in their food then any protein that they eat will not be used as protein but used to make up the calorie needs. Insufficient calorie intake is often due in children to the staple cereal being so bulky when cooked that they cannot eat enough at each meal to satisfy their needs (unless – which is unlikely – they have frequent meals).

Although suitable combinations of energy-rich foods (such as fats and oils) with protein will need to be devised, the solution to widespread under-nutrition cannot simply be a technical one. Nutrition education is meaning-less if the conditions of daily life and national economic policies allow only those who are better off to implement the knowledge acquired. Any solu-tion will not only entail a radical re-allocation of agricultural land, but also re-organised production and distribution of food. Here the experiences of China, where extensive undernutrition has been successfully overcome in the space of 25 years, are worthy of study.

Much illness and death is due to water-related infections of the 'water-washed' type (see Table 2). Any reduction in their impact requires, as well as improvements in nutrition, an increase in the quantity, availability and relia-bility of the water supply, almost irrespective of its quality. The importance of providing plenty of water close to the home cannot be over-stressed.

We may consider faecally-spread diseases and schistosomiasis together. While the effects of most of them can be substantially reduced through improved nutrition and increased quantities of easily accessible water, cer-tain of them, including schistosomiasis and hookworm, will not be elimi-nated until there are widespread adequate sewage disposal facilities. The Blair Research Laboratory in Zimbabwe has recently developed a cheap and effective pit latrine system but its success in underdeveloped countries will be limited by considerations of transport and finance, and most especi-ally by the commitment of rural people to participate in its construction and use. These latter impediments are doubtless rooted in traditional custom, justified suspicion of health authorities and ineffective community organis-ation. The solutions involve sustained campaigns undertaken by committed health teams acting with sympathetic, informed and well-organised local populations. China's experience, where there has been unprecedented success in controlling agricultural and disease-carrying pests, including the snail vector of schistosomiasis, testifies that these solutions too are funda-mentally political.

In Table 1 we included London, at the turn of the century, alongside the contemporary underdeveloped countries. The example of England and Wales is a good one to consider for it demonstrates that the disease patterns we have described are not *tropical* ones but existed in Britain not so long ago. The patterns have since changed, not as a result of great advances in medicine but because of massive social changes.

The death rates fell rapidly from the beginning of the eighteenth century to the present day in Britain, largely (over 80%) due to a fall in deaths due to infectious diseases. The decline in the number of deaths of children caused by four important infectious diseases is shown in Figure 1, and a similar graph exists for deaths from tuberculosis.

*Figure 1:   Deaths of Children Under 15 Years Old in England and Wales, Attributed to Scarlet Fever, Diphtheria, Whooping Cough and Measles, 1850-1965.*[6]

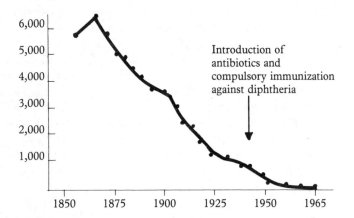

What was the background to these massive improvements in health which occurred in Britain in the nineteenth century? What relevance does this have for countries which today exhibit the disease profile of underdevelopment?

The foremost factor promoting better health in Britain was improved nutrition. Later environmental improvements, especially clean water supplies, sewage disposal and improved housing and working conditions cut down exposure to infection. Later still, effective medical treatment contributed to what was already an enormous decline in the numbers of deaths and illnesses from infectious diseases.

We cannot go deeply into the complex reasons for these changes in social conditions. But we can note that, before and during this period, the agricultural and industrial revolutions, together with the exploitation of the resources of the now underdeveloped world, led to a great concentration of

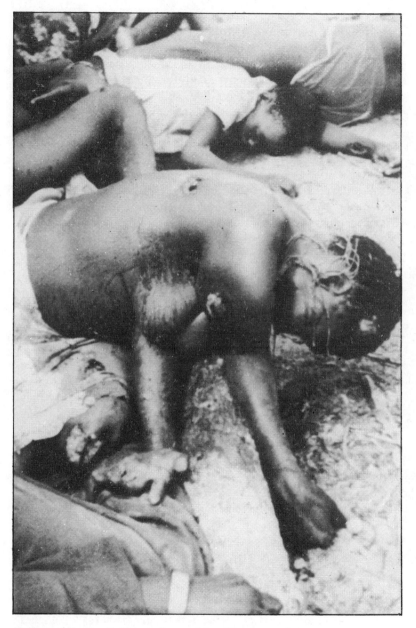

**Victims of the South African Army raid on Kassinga refugee camp**

wealth in Britain. But how was this wealth, created by the labour of the British working class and the pillage of the colonised world, distributed?

There was widespread discontent in Britain among the people who had been dispossessed of land or displaced from individual domestic production and forced to seek jobs in factories. This discontent resulted in riots and strikes which met with brutal repression but it also resulted in the formation of trade unions and other workers' movements and the emergence of social reformers such as Robert Owen and Lord Shaftesbury. These reformers pioneered the improved living conditions which, with nutrition, had such a marked impact on health.

We can see that as a result of capitalist industrial development and the struggles of working people a fundamental change in the pattern of disease and a qualitative improvement in health occurred. But new working and living conditions were created and these have thrown up new health problems. Uneven development – a fundamental characteristic of capitalist development – has brought with it new patterns of disease and disparities in health.

## D.  Can a Similar Path be Followed in Namibia?

We cannot suggest that the solution to underdevelopment in Southern Africa, or anywhere else, is capitalist development like Britain's in the eighteenth and nineteenth centuries. It is no longer possible. Control of the world's resources has become increasingly concentrated among fewer and fewer enterprises whose budgets are greater than many third world countries' national economies – including companies such as Anglo American, RTZ and others with interests in Namibia. In many underdeveloped countries foreign ownership accounts for most private capital, especially in the mining and agricultural sectors. In most such countries dependent on western capitalist markets there has been no improvement in health for the majority of the people, and in some countries (e.g. Brazil) there is evidence that the health is getting worse.

In stark contrast are the cases of China and Cuba. The people of China in the 1930s and 1940s endured widespread poverty, poor sanitation, continuing war and rampant disease. Their death rate was estimated at about 25 deaths each year per 1,000 people, one of the world's highest rates, and of every thousand babies born as many as 200 would die in their first year of life. Most deaths in China were due to infectious diseases, usually complicated by some form of malnutrition. Visitors to China now report a nation of healthy-looking vigorous people. National statistics are not yet available, but for one city, Shanghai, the death rate is down to only 6 per 1,000 and infant mortality has fallen to 9 per 1,000 – from an estimated 150 per 1,000 for Shanghai in 1948. Shanghai may not be representative of the rest of China but the remarkable changes there probably indicate rapid changes in health status throughout China. These are not the results of changes in the distribution of medical services alone: improvements in nutrition, sanitation, and general living standards have almost certainly been more important.

In Cuba, too, the achievements have been very impressive particularly when compared with nearby islands such as Haiti where disease and death rates remain high. Although health in Cuba at the time of liberation in 1959 was considerably better than it was in pre-revolutionary China the gains have been nonetheless remarkable. Diseases such as poliomyelitis, diphtheria and tuberculosis, which are endemic in Central America, have been virtually eliminated. Infant mortality has dropped in twenty years from over 60 per 1,000 to 22 per 1,000 and continues to fall.

# The Medical Contribution

## A.  Health Care Facilities

The health services in Southern African countries, as in many underdeveloped countries, are provided by a number of agencies of which the government and the religious missions are the most important. They are mainly curative medical services with only a very small percentage of budgets – usually less than 10% – being spent on preventive activities.

The institutions are largely urban based and in Southern Africa they are mostly located in 'white areas' distant from and inaccessible to the black majority. Large sophisticated units receive a disproportionate amount of the health budget so the same illness costs more to be treated in or near such units than it does in the more distant rural areas.

The high running costs of these institutions are not simply due to their size. A major expense is the higher proportion of specialists, general doctors, nurses and paramedical staff, and the costs of more expensive equipment. The cost of building and running different types of facility – a dispensary, a health centre, and a regional hospital – have been estimated to be in the ratio of 1:10:100 for capital expenditure, and 1:5:50 for running costs.[7] For example, 50 dispensaries could be run for the cost of running one regional hospital, or 10 dispensaries built for the cost of building a health centre.

Attempts to improve 'coverage' by creating a referral system have largely failed. Distance is a serious impediment to obtaining health care where transport facilities are both poor and expensive relative to average earnings. And speed is often essential to effective treatment such as the rehydration of children with diarrhoea – a common cause of death – and in complicated obstetric cases. Data from the few surveys done indicate that most patients visiting health care facilities come from the immediate vicinity. In Kenya 40% of out-patients attending a health centre lived within five miles, 70% within ten miles. Similar figures have been gathered for Tanzania and India. Use of in-patient facilities also shows a lack of referral coverage: a survey in Ghana found that 80% of the in-patients in the five major hospitals came from the surrounding urban districts. It was estimated that only about one third of Ghana's population is covered by their official health service. In Uganda, a survey in 1964 showed that of all admissions to the 'national referral' hospital in Kampala, 93% came from the surrounding district.

## B.  Personnel

All categories of health personnel are concentrated in the urban areas. This is particularly the case with doctors and nurses, but even lower level health workers are disproportionately urban-based. Indeed, during the colonial period the development of the category 'auxiliary' was prompted partly by the recognition of this tendency for professional health workers to migrate to urban areas. (The other factor was the lower cost of training and employing auxiliary staff who, it has been shown, can perform the medical interventions needed to deal with the majority of health problems. In Zimbabwe the 'medical assistant' in the hospital and clinic services, and the 'health assistant' in the preventive services are the most important categories of health care provider in rural areas.)

Although the use of auxiliaries has extended health services into areas where none were previously available, they display the same shortcomings as the professional health workers they were trained to replace. A survey in Ethiopia found that 83% of health officers did not want to work in health centres for long, and 78% wanted to study for a medical degree. Auxiliaries of all types in both Ethiopia and Tanzania frequently reveal in discussions their desire to become doctors. In Thailand, a delegation studying the health services noted that auxiliaries 'tend to stay close to their posts, even though the work there may not keep them busy'. And an extensive study in Tanzania found that both student auxiliaries and qualified auxiliaries had the same patronising approach and negative attitudes towards the rural population as their professional mentors. While figures do not exist for Zimbabwe, several reports and personal observations confirm that these same general problems exist.

## C. Summary

The colonisation of Southern Africa brought with it colonial forms of health service. These have emphasised curative medicine at the expense of preventive activities.

In most post-colonial countries the health professions and the local elites have continued and developed these western-style patterns of health service. In many cases they have adopted the educational curricula and the institutions of the former colonial power. The professionals can thus be sure of finding work abroad if they wish, and can use that fact to then demand high levels of pay. These attitudes to health and health care are transmitted to lower levels of health workers and have been the basis for their professional aspirations, urban migration and high drop-out rate.

The situation is further entrenched by medical business interests. The examples of the baby food business and the drugs suppliers and medical equipment companies have demonstrated how the use of inappropriate technology can increase the demands made on resources and also increase the distortions made in the services in the interests of a minority. Much foreign 'aid' has similar effects, often benefiting the donor more than the recipient.

The medical profession comes mainly from the higher social classes and frequently forms links with both local and international business interests, particularly in the medical field. Behind the argument of 'professional freedom' doctors insist on private practice rights, expensive facilities and equipment, and unrestricted prescribing of expensive drugs. They resist social changes that would threaten their position nationally or internationally. For example, during the brief period of Salvador Allende's left-wing government in Chile, many professionals resisted the democratisation of health care institutions.

Health professionals have spread the idea that disease in the underdeveloped world is due to 'ignorance' and 'overbreeding' rather than underdevelopment and exploitation. The medical contribution, while it is dominated by the medical profession and its allies in big business and in the government, is much more part of the problem of underdevelopment than part of its solution.

# Democracy and Health

We have argued that any qualitative improvements in health will be the result of economic and political changes which ensure the ending of the process of underdevelopment and the consequent improvement of living and working conditions for the majority. These are the responsibilities of the struggle for national liberation.

As a liberation movement develops it may create 'models', albeit embryonic, for the future provision of services and for the political involvement of the community in the running of these services. The attainment of a radically restructured health service is indivisible from, and indeed arises out of, the general political and economic achievements of the liberation movement.

The most important, and attainable, development within the health sector would be 'Mass participation in decision taking and review, and in strategy formulation and the control of leaders, as well as the implementation of projects and carrying out of decisions': in short, *democratisation and self-reliance*. A longer-term goal is to counter and eventually remove the influence of market forces on health.

Although the strategy of Primary Health Care (PHC) has been interpreted in many ways depending on the political outlook of the interpreter, the PHC strategy in its broadest sense can form the basis within the health sector for the struggle to improve health.

## A.   Primary Health Care

Let us now turn to Primary Health Care (PHC) and the role of the Community Health Worker (CHW). Two important aspects of PHC are:

☆ PHC is essential health care made universally accessible to individuals and families in the community by means acceptable to them, through their full participation and at a cost that the community and the country can afford. It forms an integral part both of the country's health system of which it is the nucleus and of the overall social and economic development of the community.

☆ PHC addresses the main health problems in the community providing promotive, preventive, curative and rehabilitative services accordingly. Since these services reflect and evolve from the economic conditions and social values of the country and its communities they will vary by country and by community, but will include at least: promotion of safe water, basic sanitation, maternal and child care including family planning, immunization against the major infectious diseases, prevention and control of locally endemic disease, education concerning prevailing health problems and the methods of preventing and controlling them, and appropriate treatment for common diseases and injuries.[8]

The implementation of PHC must not be an excuse to provide poorly resourced and less good health care for the masses. Indeed, to function effectively PHC needs specialist technical, organisational and administrative support.

Let us now consider the CHW, who is the most important PHC provider, being the living interface between the community and the formal health service.

## B. The Community Health Worker

The failure of the 'auxiliary' to meet health care needs in underdeveloped countries has already been mentioned. Because of this failure, and the contrasting success of the barefoot doctor in China, the CHW, and indeed the whole PHC strategy, has emerged. Initially these workers were involved in small-scale voluntary projects. The success of some of these projects has accelerated their development for national use in some countries, such as India. Unfortunately, their success in both China and in the earlier small schemes has not been easy to replicate on a national scale.

There are three reasons why Primary Health Care and the barefoot doctors in China were so successful. Firstly the barefoot doctors were selected during the cultural revolution in the late 1960s, by which time great advances in health due to improved social conditions had already taken place. Also, surplus wealth produced by communes was available to be allocated to health care. Thirdly, and most important of all, the democratic process allowing for selection and control of barefoot doctors already existed. For while China may not have a fully-fledged mass democracy, the democratic system is considerably advanced in comparison with many other countries.

The crucial factors distinguishing the CHW from the auxiliary are *selection* and *accountability*. In contrast to auxiliaries, CHWs are selected by the people they will serve – possibly through a representative body such as a village council or committee – and they are answerable to those people rather than to the medical profession. In the case of auxiliaries academic qualifications were the criteria used for acceptance into training, but the experience of both China and of several of the successful CHW schemes has shown that compassion and a desire to 'serve the people' may be more important qualities.

Being accountable to a community through a popularly elected body means that the elected body should be responsible for continual liaison with the CHW, constantly bringing to the CHW's attention the expressed health and health care needs of the communities s/he represents, and making known to the CHW both the satisfaction and the dissatisfaction of the people. The authority to dismiss the CHW would rest with such a body. The CHWs should be able to express through these elected bodies their ideas about how the communities or particular individuals can be involved in health promotion and health care activities.

Technical supervision and support of CHWs may in the first instance come from auxiliaries or other PHC professionals. Personnel at district and provincial levels will also have to be supportive and supervisory although – as with all PHC workers – they should have regular contact and dialogue with the popularly elected representative bodies. Only through such a dialogue will those assuming responsibility for health services improve their understanding of what most people perceive to be their needs for health and health services. And, by engaging in such a dialogue, health workers can demonstrate their concern and their readiness to put their skills at the disposal of the community – a community whose active participation in health promotion and disease control is crucial.

Who pays for the CHW? It is important that the workload of the CHWs should not stop them spending some of their time in other productive activities. This will ensure that CHWs do not become full-time health workers, dependent only on their skills for their living and potentially open to the attractions of private practice; and being involved in the same productive work as the people they serve will ensure that they remain close in perceptions and experience to those people. By being part-time CHWs, the payment needed is only a subsidy rather than a full-time wage. There will be poor rural (and urban) communities which cannot generate even small subsidies for their CHWs, but if CHWs are to remain answerable to their communities then it is important that whatever subsidy is found – e.g. from national funds – it should be *administered* by the community or their elected representatives.

## C.   The Role of the Community Health Worker

We can now examine the role of the CHWs and how they can help promote self-reliance and help their communities attain good health.

Health workers based in the community can extend health care to many people who would otherwise derive little benefit from the health services.

The use of simple technologies can greatly enhance the CHW's ability to prevent and cure disease and ease suffering. Equipping a CHW with curative skills not only provides health care to more people, more quickly and more cheaply, but also gives the CHW greater credibility in the eyes of the community. And if the CHW can give members of the community both an understanding of and some skills in health care then the medical profession's monopoly of knowledge and expertise is challenged. The power of the doctor, often based on mystification, can in this way be democratized. The widespread use of simple technologies can also stimulate a critical approach to the present sophisticated, expensive and mystifying technologies. In this way *conscious self reliance* can be fostered, that is self-reliance based on knowledge rather than something imposed on a passive and unconscious community.

But perhaps the most important potential of CHWs is their ability to stimulate within the health sector the growth of a movement for progressive social change – to act as an agent of social change. As David Werner has written:

> If the village health worker is taught a respectable range of skills, if he* is encouraged to think, to take the initiative and to keep learning on his own if his judgement is respected, if his limits are determined by what he knows and can do, if his supervision is supportive and educational, chances are he will work with energy and dedication, will make a major contribution to his community and will win his people's confidence and love. His example will serve as a role model to his neighbours, that they too can learn new skills and assume new responsibilities, that self-improvement is possible. Thus the village health worker becomes an internal agent-of-change, not only for health care but for the awakening of his people to their human potential . . . and ultimately to their human rights.'[9]

The CHW's special qualification to be an agent of social change comes from two sources both equally important. First, through the mechanisms of selection and payment, CHWs are more likely to represent their community rather than the medical profession or the state. Second, CHWs can, with assistance, build up a picture of the social roots of ill-health in their area, and so endorse people's ideas that their ill-health derives from their living and working conditions. Contrary to many misguided assumptions, villagers do know

---

* Editors' note: In both this quotation and the next one, David Werner has implied that CHWs (or VHWs) are usually male. In Southern Africa they are more likely to be female. The view expressed – that their primary role is to lead their community in resisting oppression – thus applies with even greater strength.

that disease is caused by food (or its lack), bad sanitation and hygiene, poor water supplies, excessive work and bodily weakness. If the CHWs are regarded by communities as their representatives and are respected for their responsiveness and caring skills, then they can have a powerful effect in confirming communities' understanding of the sources of their ill-health.

A good example of this potential of the CHW is given by David Werner, considering the possible approaches to diarrhoea:

'Each year millions of peasant children die of diarrhoea. We tend to agree that most of these deaths could be prevented. Yet diarrhoea remains the number one killer of infants in Latin America and much of the developing world. Does this mean our so-called preventive measures are merely palliative? At what point in the chain of causes which makes death from diarrhoea a global problem . . . are we coming to grips with the real underlying cause? Do we do it . . .

. . . by preventing some deaths through treatment of diarrhoea?

. . . by trying to interrupt the infectious cycle through construction of latrines and water systems?

. . . by reducing high risk from diarrhoea through better nutrition?

. . . by curbing land tenure inequalities through land reform?

Land reform comes closest to the real problem. But the peasantry is oppressed by far more inequities than those of land tenure. Both causing and perpetuating these crushing inequities looms the existing power structure: local, national, foreign and multinational. It includes political, commercial and religious power groups as well as the legal profession and the medical establishment. In short, it includes . . . ourselves . . .

Where, then, should prevention begin? Beyond doubt, anything we can do to minimize the inequities perpetuated by the existing power structure will do far more to reduce high infant mortality than all our conventional preventive measures put together. We should, perhaps, carry on with our latrine-building rituals, nutrition centres and agricultural extension projects. But let's stop calling it prevention. We are still only treating symptoms. And unless we are very careful, we may even be making the underlying problem worse . . . through increasing dependency on outside aid, technology and control.

But this need not be the case. *If* the building of latrines brings people together and helps them look ahead, *if* a nutrition centre is built and run by the community and fosters self-reliance, and *if* agricultural extension, rather than imposing outside technology encourages internal growth of the people towards more effective understanding and use of their land, their potential and their rights . . . then, and only then, do latrines, nutrition centres and so-called extension work begin to deal with the real causes of preventable sickness and death.

This is where the village health worker comes in. It doesn't matter much if he spends more time treating diarrhoea than building latrines. Both are merely palliative in view of the larger problem. What matters is that he gets his people together.

Yes, the most important role of the village health worker *is* preventive. But preventive in the fuller sense, in the sense that he help his people, as individuals and as a community, liberate themselves not only from outside exploitation and oppression, but from their own short-sightedness, futility and greed.

The chief role of the village health worker, at his best, is that of liberator.'[10]

And this ideal, the liberating potential of the CHW, the people's representative, is quite the opposite of the negative potential of many health professionals who transmit the idea that social conditions causing ill-health are natural and unchangeable and that any solutions rest with the individual.

## D. Problems for Community Health Worker Schemes

While some schemes involving CHWs have proved very successful other attempts have failed. There are several reasons for this failure, some specific to certain schemes and others common to many of them. Here we discuss some more general problems that CHW schemes may encounter:

*Economic:* In China, even now, in bad agricultural years the funds for rural health programmes are reduced. In countries with poor communities, where production is mostly on an individual basis, there is frequently no surplus in the community to subsidise a CHW. And even where a surplus has been created, poor people understandably choose to invest in items which they regard as more vital than health care. They often choose to invest in land or farm machinery, which undoubtedly contribute more to their general health than health care. In Mozambique a new category of health worker, the *agente polivalente*, has been created who works in the communal villages, but in some villages there has been too little communal production to support the *agente*, who then has to spend most of his/her time producing essential food for the family.

Most of the successful CHW schemes either receive substantial funding from a non-governmental (usually foreign) agency, or, after an initial period of reliance on such outside funding, they have devised workable health insurance schemes. But whether such schemes can be sustained depends in the long term on how much surplus is produced within the community and who controls it. In the early phases it may be necessary for governments to provide central funding for a CHW scheme. It is important, though, that such funds be administered by local representative bodies, bodies which are in fact the employers of the CHWs.

*Political:* Popular, democratic control is a crucial ingredient for the success of a primary health care scheme based on CHWs. In communities where most people are poor and often illiterate the tendency is for better-off and better-educated individuals to dominate in the decision-making process. This has implications for both the selection and control of the community-based health worker. It calls into question the very notion of 'community', a term which is very freely used and which suggests a homogeneous, conflict-free group of people. This is almost never the case. Observations on the social structure of villages in India suggest that the rich landlords take the benefits brought by the new health workers and allow very little to reach those most in need of them – the village councils are dominated by the land-lords and so the selection of health workers by the 'community' merely means selection dominated by local vested interests.

A contribution to a UNICEF publication devoted to primary health care noted:

> The unhappy reality in many developing countries is that unless the structure of privileges and highly unequal social and economic relation-ships among the people are swept away by prior change in the national political structure, the creation of a community spirit, the articulation of community aspirations, the people's participation in the planning and management of community programmes can progress only falteringly and in limited ways.
>
> Projects are often cited as examples of community participation in situations where the national political system has not yet established the basis of cohesive communities and has not removed the barriers to com-munity participation; however sometimes a closer examination reveals that even in these projects, community participation merely means giving a voice in local decisions to the local influential people, rather than to the most needy and the deprived who may constitute the majority. It may also be found that a disproportionately small share of the services and benefits go to the neediest. In other instances, community participation means seeking the local people's compliance with predetermined central plans

and programmes, and extracting financial and other contributions from them rather than a genuine partnership between the government agency and the people.'[11]

Where the old order and previous power structures have been – or are still being – contested the primary health care schemes involving CHWs are likely to take root. In such circumstances popular participation in decision-making and collective self-reliance may grow and flourish.

★　★　★　★　★

This chapter has shown how a population's health reflects its country's social and economic development and the distribution of political power. The politics and economics of Southern Africa determine the health, and hence the health care needs, of the people. They also determine the nature of the formal health service. Overcoming the gap between people's health needs and the sort of service provided will both reflect and reinforce the general process of social development. It will be upon this general process of social development in turn that the possibility of improved health will finally depend.

## References

1 SWAPO and WHO *Country Health Programming for an Independent Namibia* Lusaka, 1980.
2 *Ibid.*
3 Adapted from figures given by J Rohde 'The Parsons Lecture' University of Birmingham Medical School, 1982.
4 Adapted from D J Bradley *Human Rights in Health* CIBA Foundation Symposium 23 (New Series), Elsevier Amsterdam, 1984.
5 Country Health Programming, *op. cit.*
6 Cited in J Gilmurray, R Riddell and D Sanders *The Struggle for Health* CIIR, 1979. Similar figures may be found in T McKeown *The Role of Medicine* The Nuffield Provincial Hospitals Trust, 1976.
7 O Gish *Guidelines for Health Planners* Tri-Med Books, 1977.
8 WHO/UNICEF *Primary Health Care* Alma Ata, 1978.
9 D Werner *The Village Health Worker – Lackey or Liberator* The Hesperian Foundation, 1977 (mimeo).
10 *Ibid.* See also D Werner's *Health Care and Human Dignity.*
11 M Ahmed 'Community Participation – The Heart of Primary Health Care' *Assignment Children* UNICEF, 1978.

# 5

# Health Workers in their Political and Social Context

No-one knows better than the people of Namibia that a declaration of independence – or even an armed revolution – is only the first step towards the liberation of the people. Even after the foreign occupiers have been driven out many forces of oppression will continue to operate.

The process of liberation is not just one of armed struggle or political decree. It is one of gradual social transformation, an educational group process in which individuals learn to live and work together both *freely* and *fairly*:

☆ *freely* in the sense that each nation, each community and each family group is free to become self-reliant and to make independent decisions on matters concerning their well-being;

☆ *fairly* in the sense that groups of people, small and large, learn to prevent peacefully any member of that group (or an outsider) from seeking control or privilege at the expense of others.

In short, liberation is a continuing collective process to defend basic rights.

Where do health workers fit into this? That will depend on many factors – mostly political.

In Namibia, SWAPO has declared its intention to restructure the health system to meet the needs of all the people. This is coupled with an overall commitment towards achieving greater equity in the socio-economic and political sectors. Thus the political climate is – or will be – in favour of selecting and training health workers who will serve rather than take advantage of the people.

There are many obstacles to attaining this goal. Some useful insights can be gained by considering the experiences of other countries that have gained independence or undergone popular revolution.

## Mexico

The last Mexican Revolution took place between 1910 and 1917. This resulted in a remarkable, socially progressive constitution for its time. An amendment in 1934 guaranteed to all Mexicans a basic right to health. Since then many rural development programmes have been launched: roads, schools, and more recently agriculture and health extension work. Programme after programme to 'bring health to the rural areas' has been tried – and has failed. First, graduating medical students were obliged to perform a year of rural service. This proved inadequate, so attempts were made to train village health aides and auxiliary nurses. When these gave poor results a massive effort was made to place young doctors in 2,000 prefabricated, absolutely standardized rural health posts set up with what was imaginatively called 'community participation'. But communities were often unco-operative and many doctors went absent or became corrupt. The impact on health proved marginal and in some ways negative: previous measures were mostly neglected and the misuse or overuse of medications was horrendous!

Today the Ministry of Health is about to launch a new programme with two levels of village health workers. They will have 2 weeks training for villages of under 500 people, and 3 months training for larger villages.

Will this succeed? The success of health workers at community level depends on how much responsibility the people themselves take – or are permitted to take – for their own well-being. In Mexico there is tight central control by a single political party – the so-called Institutionalized Revolutionary Party. Although it has a face of social reform it in fact represents the interests of a powerful minority of large land owners, industrialists, politicians and professionals – including doctors.

Effective community health work involves community awareness and decision-making. It involves popular organisation. If common people join together to gain greater control over their own health this is the beginning of an awakening. They may begin to organise to gain more control over things such as land, production, and decisions that affect their lives. This would, of course, be a threat to those in power. Therefore care is taken that agriculture and health extension work create dependence on government assistance rather than promoting true self-reliance. The goal is to calm any unrest.

Community health workers are selected and trained in such a way that they feel greater allegiance to those in power than to those in need. It is no accident that the 'tasks' of community health workers are rigidly and narrowly defined, nor that they must wear uniforms to look like an outside authority, nor that they spend their time filling out endless forms. Care is taken to make them subservient and unquestioning.

If in Mexico the latest plan for reaching the rural population through the training of village health workers once again goes amiss, it will be because those in positions of control have been afraid to distribute political power. They fear the chain of events that might take place if rural and working people are permitted to organise and take charge of factors that determine their health.


## Central America

Similar stories can be written for many other countries in Latin America – and maybe much of the underdeveloped world. *Governments that do not represent the people train health workers that do not represent the people.* Governments take such strategic precautions for they know well that non-government, community-based health workers have in many countries played a key role in accelerating social transformation. In Nicaragua many courageous *promotores de salud* (health promotors) became village organisers in the struggle that led to the overthrow of the Somoza dictatorship. In Guatemala and El Salvador, village health workers have become prime targets of 'disappearances' and have been tortured by military and paramilitary forces. In Guatemala it has reached the point where to be caught with a first aid pamphlet can be a crime punishable by death.

Health workers at every level, from doctors to village aides, can be important political agents – either for or against the people. Following independence or a popular revolution one might suppose that both the health ministry and its health workers would work to help the people gain more power and control over their own health. But it is rarely so simple.


## China

We can compare the health systems of China and Cuba. Both have an egalitarian political philosophy with a clear commitment to 'health for all'. China's creation of the 'barefoot doctor' was not just an appropriate, low-cost measure to provide health care at the village or commune level. It was a political act to take the control of health care out of the hands of the medical establishment and place it back into the hands of the people. Medical schools were for a time closed down and doctors were sent for rotations into the rural areas – not just to serve the people and train barefoot doctors, but to blister their hands doing farm work. Most important, the barefoot doctors were selected by their commune, paid by their commune, and answerable directly to their commune. Thus control over health care was to a large extent decentralised. With other egalitarian policies China has achieved a vast overall improvement in the health status of ¼ of the world's people, in only a few years and without significant foreign aid.

## Cuba

Cuba, like China, has remarkably improved the health of its people since the Revolution of 1959. But Cuba has done so very differently and at a much higher cost per person, with a massive programme to train more doctors and set up an extensive network of 'polyclinics' and rural hospitals delivering health care to the entire population. Thus the first level of health care in Cuba, as in many Western industrialised countries, is directly to doctors and medical specialists in clinics and hospitals. There are community health workers, but their main role is to collect information and to refer patients to the nearest health facility.

Control of health care remains largely in the hands of the medical profession and the Ministry of Health. Although the health of Cubans has increased dramatically, so has the cost of health care, and so has the people's dependence on professionals.

Why, we may ask, did Cuba's revolutionaries reform rather than restructure the health system? Why was the medical monopoly left intact, and even strengthened?

One reason may lie in the crisis in the health services precipitated at the Revolution. At the time of the liberation many of the doctors in Cuba fled the country. The new government was in a desperate situation with a well-established service in the urban areas on the verge of collapse. It reinstated into the new Health Ministry some of the same doctors who had held positions in the pre-revolutionary Batista dictatorship. It is a point to emphasise, because it is a position many newly-liberated countries have had to adopt.

## Nicaragua

Nicaragua, upon the overthrow of Somoza, was also faced with an exodus of physicians and the new Ministry of Health was formed in part by the leading physicians who remained. The Sandinista government was at first determined to restructure totally the health service as had been done in China, in order to emphasise primary care and the training of community health workers.

With the acute shortage of medical personnel, however, hundreds of Cuban doctors were invited in, not only to fill the gap but to serve as advisors in planning the new health system. The Cuban doctors recommended the same approach as had been applied in Cuba, removing much of the community base of health care.

The community health workers in Nicaragua were, however, already fairly well organised. Many had been popular leaders and community guerilla medics during the struggle. They continued to work with the new Ministry of Health but made it clear that they were accountable first to their communities.

For example, when a team of Mexican village health workers was in Nicaragua in 1982 conducting a training course on teaching methods the local health workers suddenly received orders from the Ministry of Health to change their plans and interrupt the course. The health workers replied that they would always consider seriously any suggestions from the Ministry of Health, but that they took their orders from the community. The community Committee for the Defense of the Revolution voted not to interrupt the course and the health workers followed the community's request.

The fact that the local community and its health workers had the courage to stand up to the health ministry is impressive. The fact that the ministry then accepted their decision is even more encouraging and gives hope that in time there will be even greater decentralized control and a stronger community base. It already seems to be happening: within the last year an official decision has been made to give high priority to the training of several new levels of community workers.

## Zimbabwe

The complex situation in post-independent Zimbabwe cannot be easily summarised. The incoming Ministry of Health faced a medical profession still dominated by the pre-independence establishment: the Medical Council, the Medical School and the extensive, prosperous private medical services. The budget was dominated by the urban-based, curative hospitals with little being spent on rural health care. Rural services had been badly disrupted during the war, and what remained were largely run by the church missions.

The Health Ministry has attempted to take gradual control of both rural and urban services with a policy of reform rather than radical restructuring. Health care is now free for those with low incomes: but access to health facilities is only slowly extending to the more deprived areas. Guerilla medics faced great obstacles in being integrated into the medical services: an example can be given where they were being re-trained ('upgraded') in rural programmes by mission staff. A visitor to one such upgrading course – run by an elderly German doctor – reported that he expected to find a spirited group committed to continuing the struggle for their people's rights:

'Are there still many people in Zimbabwe who are hungry?' he asked the class of ex-guerilla health workers.

'Oh yes, many,' they replied.

'Why?'

'Because the people are lazy,' some answered. 'Because they are ignorant.' 'Because they don't like work.' 'Because they drink...' All of these are answers one might expect from oppressed people who have been taught to blame only themselves for their problems. How could they be saying such things so soon after being in the liberation armies?

One young woman spoke out and said 'Not true! Our people are hungry because all the good land is still in the hands of a few wealthy owners. The poor people have been pushed onto land that is worthless. They are forced to work on the large plantations at starvation wages. They are herded together into tiny shacks. If they drink it is because...'

At this point she was interrupted by the German doctor. 'I'm sorry,' the doctor apologised to the visitor. 'You must remember that these people are all cowards who ran away and fought against their country. But I am slowly retraining them.'

## Mozambique

Soon after Mozambique's liberation the new Ministry of Health nationalised all health services, abolished private medical practice, and made the rural areas its first priority. From a discriminatory, curative, urban-oriented service a national network of health units has been developed, with a focus on prevention and participation.

Based on the *socorristas* of Frelimo's armed struggle, the training of village health workers was given high priority at independence. They were trained outside the national health institutes, in small provincial schools and health centres near to the communities they were to serve. They were selected by the villagers, trained for six months and then returned to their homes to provide simple preventive and curative services. People they cannot help are referred to the nearest health centre. They are not paid by the health service but by their own communities, although their drugs are provided by the national service. In theory they were to be allocated to the communal villages, and they were to work half-time as health workers and half-time in collective production. In practice, the uneven development of communal villages in Mozambique has meant that the idea was ahead of its time, and some villages were unable to support their health worker from their own surplus production. As a result some health workers have returned to farming, while others have returned to providing a service on state farms rather than communal villages.

**Refugee camp in Angola**

There have also been difficulties in transport, particularly during the rainy season, compounded by a lack of vehicles, problems of maintenance and the poor condition of many roads – problems all made more difficult by the continuing disruption caused by the so-called Mozambique National Resistance (MNR). Village health workers, despite these difficulties, are highly valued by their communities and are seen as a vital link with the rest of the health services.

Another feature of Mozambique's health care is the major attempt to democratise the running of the hospital services by the creation of ward councils, first in Maputo Hospital and later in all hospitals. Substituting colonial power with popular power was not enough: colonial structures within the hospitals had to be changed by establishing democratic ward councils, organising ways for patients to criticise and make suggestions about the running of the hospitals, and improving worker education facilities. As President Samora Machel, himself trained as a nurse, has written:

> Our hospitals belong to the people. They are a fruit of the revolution. Our hospitals are far more than centres for dispensing medicines and cures. A Frelimo hospital is a centre where our political line – that of serving the masses – is put into practice.[1]

The hospital is a state institution where Party policy touches the most sensitive points of the population: health, well-being and life itself. It is often in the hospital that the people see reflected the organisation of our State. It is there that the people feel directly the fruits of independence and of the construction of socialism.[2]

Mozambique continues to face considerable problems. Internal defence against the MNR costs Mozambique a third of its national budget. The MNR have destroyed over 200 rural health posts and severely disrupted services, while the country has suffered the worst drought for many years. And there is no certainty that conditions will improve in the near future.

## Serving the People

The first section of this chapter has dealt with a variety of different countries and summarised a few of the salient features of those countries' health care systems. We will now move on to try and draw some general conclusions from the broad experiences of those countries and others that have achieved independence or liberation from colonial occupation.

As we have seen, the approach to restructuring such a country's health system varies widely, as does the role of the health workers produced. Generally, the health system reflects the social structure of the country, and the health professionals represent that system. In particular, if they are selected and paid by the government, they will represent the government, and if the government does not represent the needs of the people, then nor will they.

What can we learn from this that might help select and train health workers to best serve the people freely and fairly?

### Health Workers in a Society in Transition

A country may become 'free' at one particular moment, but its people become free from oppression slowly. Oppression exists not only in the international and national context but also 'closer to home'. Each village and each family group may have its oppressors and its oppressed. Individuals can even be oppressed – or depressed – by their own low opinion of themselves, their own lack of confidence and loss of hope. All this takes time to change. And if it does not change then national liberation will be shallow and cannot last. There are always people looking for power and privilege who are waiting their chance to manoeuvre and take over. Unless the least powerful learn to organise and defend their interest then the new oppressors and new forms of oppression can emerge.

Health workers can become leaders of change by helping those most subject to oppression gain the confidence, skills, understanding and organisation they need to safeguard their health and their rights. But health workers can do this better if the government's health system is re-structured in a decentralized, people-supportive way.

Here are some suggestions for structuring a people-centred health system:

1. Tip the 'health workers pyramid' (see the diagram) onto its side so that the community comes first and is no longer at the bottom. Have community health workers together with mothers, schoolchildren and other community members play the lead role in health care, so that the medical professionals become the auxiliaries: on tap and not on top.

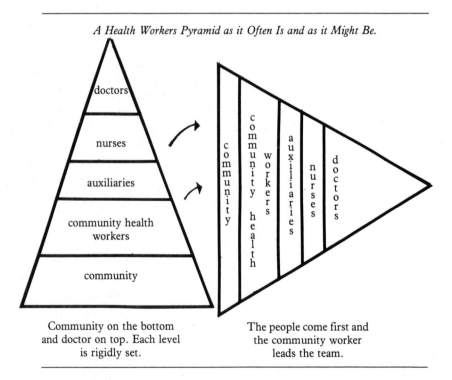

*A Health Workers Pyramid as it Often Is and as it Might Be.*

Community on the bottom and doctor on top. Each level is rigidly set.

The people come first and the community worker leads the team.

2. Make the largest, most important body of health workers be community or village health workers. Invest more in training and providing for community health workers than for doctors.

3. Be sure that community health workers are selected by, representative of, and are responsible to the poorer, or more oppressed, members of the community. (This may be an argument for having more women health workers than men.)

4. Explore alternatives for ensuring that the local health workers are accountable first to their own community. Thus consider:
   ☆ Whether they should be paid or voluntary, full or part time?
   ☆ Whether they can be paid or sustained by the community rather than depending on central government for all health care?

5. Ensure that the Ministry of Health acts as a co-ordinator, supplier and advisor, rather than a 'controller' of the community health workers. As far as possible, control and supervision should come from the community and involve a democratic group process.

6. Formulate a national health plan that is flexible and innovative rather than rigidly standardized. Try different approaches in different geographic areas, following the suggestions of local people.

7. Encourage all health workers to take initiatives, be innovative, and feel responsible for both applying and improving the health plan. The mistakes made by health workers responding to innovative challenges are not nearly so dangerous as the apathy and corruption that can result from turning health workers into disheartened civil servants.

8. Build into the national health plan an easy avenue for all people, including health workers, to participate in continually evaluating and redesigning the plan. Encourage criticisms and suggestions – *no plan or policy or official should be sacred or above criticism*. Encourage health workers to be the vigilantes of people's rights.

9. For the training – or, better, *education* – of health workers at all levels, use methods of non-formal education that will help them share their knowledge openly, treat other people as equals, and become leaders for change.

## Health Professionals as Auxiliaries to Community Workers

We discussed the role of community health workers first because this is where a people-based health system might devote its main energies and funds. However, doctors and other health professionals are also important – although expensive and often unwilling to serve where and how they are needed.

In a health system designed to serve all the people there need be relatively few doctors – and these must be of a breed different from most. New ways must be worked out to select and train such doctors: doctors who are not supermen or superwomen, but are down-to-earth, ordinary people ...

... who regard themselves as equal to everybody else.

... who are willing to share their knowledge and explain things so that everyone understands.

... who are willing to work for earnings proportional to those of most of the people.

... who feel prevention is the key but who respect the people's urgency for curative care.

... who are good teachers, story tellers, and listeners.

... who have a basic understanding of the health needs of the country and how these relate to sociopolitical factors.

... who are willing to learn from lesser trained (but often more experienced) persons than themselves.

... who respect traditional forms of healing and help build on them.

... who use only essential western medicines and in a cautious, sensible and economic way.

... who see their main role as being assistants to community health workers – not their bosses or superiors.

... who are committed to social justice, to building a new and fairer society.

Doctors such as these do exist. But they are the exception rather than the rule. What can be done to create doctors who are more likely to serve the people? In part, that depends on *selection*.

Selection of medical students (and doctors for government positions) should be based on human and social qualities more than wealth, influence and academic grades. Preference might be given to persons from poor rural families. For this, academic entry requirements may have to be lowered and more basic educational background provided in the first years.

In one experimental programme in the Philippines, a 'stepladder' approach is taken to the training of health workers and doctors. First, the villages select candidates to be health workers, who then train for several months and return to serve their villages. If they perform well their communities recommend them for further training, this time to be nurse-midwives. Again they return to serve their villages for a time. Next, if the villages recommend, they can train as paramedics, and then as doctors. This 'stepladder' approach has run into problems – mainly because the political climate in the Philippines is not conducive to general popular control. In a country with an egalitarian political will, however, it might succeed.

**Medical school training** needs to be evaluated critically and restructured according to the newly defined role of the doctor and the priority needs in the country. For everything taught the question needs to be asked:

> How necessary is this course? How much will the subject matter help in a small hospital or a health post to provide adequate care for most of the people's problems? What other subjects might be more useful?

If we ask questions like this, courses in dissection of the cadaver might be largely replaced by courses in the anatomy of the village. Courses in biochemistry might be replaced by courses in the misuse and overuse, and comparative costs, of medication or herbal medicines. Courses in rare diseases might be replaced by courses in communication and teaching methods.

**Locations for learning** should, as far as possible, be situations similar to where the doctor will work – i.e. a small rural hospital in preference to a large urban teaching hospital.

In Mexico City an interesting experiment is being tried, in which groups of first year medical students are transplanted from the medical school to the heart of the huge slum city of Nezahualcoyotl. On the first day the students are sent out to the poorest neighbourhoods to find 15 families for whom they will become 'health assistants' throughout the year. On the third day they make contact with another 15 families. Two days each week they visit these families, trying to help them work out how best to manage their health problems. In this way the students confront the limitations of poverty, shortage of health facilities, people's fear of hospitals, problems of bribes and corruption, and other basic facts of life than most medical students have never dreamed of. During their 'classes' on the remaining days the students try to learn from their instructors, their books, and in whatever way they can about how to help the families they visit to solve their medical, health, nutritional, and other needs. Thus the main content of the year's courses is progressively planned around the problems the students confront in the community. Theoretical studies are added when they are needed by the students, to help them gain more understanding of the problems they confront.

So far, only the first year of medical school is committed to this approach. The rest is conventional. Yet the impact that the experiment has had on the students who have participated has been tremendous. Many have gone on to be leaders in community health programmes and popular organisations. Given the present political climate in Mexico the experimental course has had difficulty surviving, in spite of – or perhaps because of – its success.

**Teaching methods** should be consistent: the methods used for training doctors should match the methods used by doctors and others to train community health workers, and in turn the methods used to train the community workers should match the methods they use to share their knowledge with villagers. These methods should encourage:

☆ more equality between instructors and students, with criticism that goes both ways.
☆ fewer lectures, more discussion, more first-hand investigation and problem solving.
☆ less memorising, more learning how to look things up.
☆ imaginative use of role-playing, storytelling and group learning games.
☆ learning by doing – less in the classroom, more in and from the community.

We will explore some specific teaching and learning methods based on these principles in Chapter 9.

### References

1 S Machel *Sowing the Seeds of Revolution*, Committee for Freedom in Angola and Mozambique: London, 1974.
2 S Machel *Reforcemos o Poder Popular nos Nossos Hospitais*, in Colecçao Palavras de Ordem, Frelimo: Maputo, 1979.

# Re-organising health care

The six parts of this chapter each examine various aspects of health and consider how health care might be extended into deprived areas. As Dr Iyambo Indongo, SWAPO Secretary for Health and Social Welfare, indicates in the *Foreword*, SWAPO has a policy of developing Primary Health Care in order to ensure 'Health for All'. Primary Health Care can take different forms, and this section opens by asking questions the planners of the new services might ask themselves as they set about their planning tasks.

This is followed by short sections on specific topics: Water and Sanitation; Maternal and Child Health; Nutrition; Oral Health; and Rehabilitation. The list of topics is not complete but the sections indicate the sorts of problems that Namibia might face, and the sorts of solutions that have been tried, when attempting to implement Primary Health Care for All in its widest sense.

The questions raised and the suggestions proposed are not meant to be prescriptive for SWAPO, but are offered in the spirit of a contribution and a resource for an independent government to use.

## PART ONE: Organising Primary Health Care

The opportunity to make great changes in the provision of health care services will be enormous. This section looks at the sort of questions that might need to be given priority at Namibia's independence.

Improving health and reducing the inequalities between different groups in Namibia will depend largely on changes outside the health service. There are many illnesses, however, where an appropriate health care service can prevent their occurrence or reduce the chances of a serious disability developing. As we discussed in Chapters 4 and 5, an appropriate health service can also be a way of involving people in decisions which intimately affect their lives.

The most urgent priority will be the extension of services to deprived communities, mostly far from the urban and industrial centres. The word 'extension' can imply an expansion of the same sort of services found in the better-off areas and this may need to be questioned. Rather than extending the services, we could say they need to be *re-oriented* in their approach and thereby *re-organised* in practice.

There are several issues to take into account when planning a re-oriented health service and when implementing these plans as a re-organised service following independence. Turning policies into practice needs to take account of:

☆ the organisation of the health services that have been developed by SWAPO for Namibian refugees and others displaced from Namibia by the war;

☆ the 'traditional' forms of health and social and cultural organisations of Namibians;

☆ the structure of services that exist in occupied Namibia.

There will, of course, be many other constraints, including the state of the national economy and the funds available for specific projects.

The 1980 document *A Country Health Programme for Independent Namibia*, published by SWAPO and the World Health Programme (WHO), identified the priority health problems for Namibia (see also Chapter 4 in this book). It found that many of the problems were amenable to preventive and promotive health activities rather than high technology curative care. A policy of Primary Health Care (PHC) has already been discussed as the most hopeful approach to reducing the burden of health problems in Namibia. The present health services for the urban elite are predominantly directed towards high technology curative care which is heavily dependent on doctor-directed services. If the policy of PHC is to be implemented then decisions have to be taken about the best use of the resources concentrated in urban areas – such as the Keetmanshoop State Hospital – and how they can be redeployed to support the extension of the formal services into rural areas to support the PHC strategy.

In Zimbabwe, following the decision of the incoming leadership to retain in the country as many of the skilled and professional (mostly white) elite as possible, there has been some difficulty in finding the resources to develop a full PHC programme while maintaining (and even increasing) the resources allocated to the central, curative services. Some resources have been found for PHC, but these have come from external agencies such as UNICEF, WHO and non-governmental organisations which have their own priorities and strategies and which offer project-funding for a limited period. When that period is over there is a danger that the government will not be able to take financial responsibility to continue the projects. The government itself has allocated funds by the simple expedient of increasing public expenditure, but such increased spending on social welfare programmes have since been squeezed by the International Monetary Fund.

With a limited budget and a range of things to spend the budget on, a decision about priorities must be taken. If PHC is a high priority then the reduction or discontinuation of some curative urban services, or at least a freeze in their growth, may be necessary. Decisions to redistribute resources should be made before independence and a timetable worked out even if implementation is delayed for practical reasons. If there is a lack of clarity at independence then an incoming government will find itself under immediate and increasing pressure to continue what already exists to the detriment of overall improvement of health care in the country. The pressures coming from vested interests need to be countered when they first arise, and the government's policies can be reinforced with visible popular mobilisation demanding resources for a re-oriented, re-organised health service.

Simply to re-name a central hospital as a referral hospital – a 'national referral centre' for the whole population – would, of course, be meaningless if the majority have little or no access to it through their local health services. As we discussed in Chapter 4, the experience of several African countries shows that such central facilities provide medical care largely for those living nearby. Zimbabwe is among those countries having problems. At independence the prestigious and enormously expensive Andrew Fleming Hospital (since renamed the Parirenyatwa Hospital) in Harare was declared to be a national referral hospital, yet even four years later 40% of the patients are not referrals but are admitted through private consultants and the medical school.

Before considering specific instances of the type of decisions that may have to be taken let us first consider some more general issues that follow the PHC strategy, a strategy which fulfills SWAPO's policy emphasising an *equitable provision of health services* combined with a *high degree of popular involvement in decisions* – decisions concerning types of services to be provided, their implementation and their management.

For each of these aspects of PHC there are questions which can be raised about planning the re-oriented health service in an independent Namibia.

## 1. Community Participation

As has been made clear in SWAPO's policy statements a central tenet of effective primary care is the involvement of people in decisions regarding their own health. Where PHC has been most successful we find there are mechanisms for popular involvement and mobilisation of people in making decisions, and not merely implementing a centrally determined plan. In Mozambique, this has drawn heavily upon the experiences of FRELIMO during the independence war and later the party political organisation.

In Namibia it will be important to identify the appropriate local structures through which this involvement and mobilisation can be achieved. This is not, of course, a question in the health sector alone, but will follow from government decisions regarding decentralisation and the devolution and delegation of power to local representative bodies.

*What local structures in Namibia will be most appropriate to ensure and encourage continuing local involvement in decisions relevant to people's lives?*

Community participation has little meaning unless there is control at local level over the expenditure of resources.

*Should and will local authorities be able to raise money for projects themselves?*

*Will they be able to decide their own priorities?*

*If they receive financial support from central government will they have control over how the money is spent?*

Health programmes involve many other sectors: sanitation and water supplies, nutrition and agricultural extension, the provision of housing and land, and increasing literacy.

*How will health planning and management fit into local administrative structures?*

*Will there be special health committees at local level?*

*Will health workers of all types meet together often enough to make common decisions regarding practice?*

*How will health workers influence and be influenced by workers in other sectors?*

## 2. Equal Access to Health Services

An essential theme of primary health care is that there should be equality of access to facilities irrespective of geographical location and social circumstances. The existing services in Namibia are extremely inequitable. SWAPO's health policy identifies a regional system of formal services to be developed in support of PHC. The formal services provided at present come largely from Church missions. In other adjacent countries this was also the case prior to independence. But the objectives of missions and other non-governmental organisations providing health care in rural areas are not always the same objectives as those of local communities. The future role of missions and other bodies providing health care will have to be considered.

*What mechanisms will be implemented to ensure that missions and non-governmental organisations follow the overall aims of PHC and comply with locally-expressed needs and decisions?*

Mining companies have provided specific health services for their contract labour. Mining will continue to be extremely important for development after independence.

*Will contract labour cease?*

*If so, will families join the male workers – and what changes in service would then be needed?*

*How much control will the new government want to exercise over these essentially independent health services?*

*What arrangements can ensure that mining companies provide appropriate health care for their workers and their families within the health policies of SWAPO?*

We have already noted the extremely inequitable provision of services at present.

*Which of the existing, mainly urban, hospital services are inappropriate to the priority health needs of the majority of Namibians – and how might these be made more accessible or else discontinued?*

Private medical practice is mainly concentrated in the urban areas and by its nature is restricted to the existing socio-economic elite.

*What controls on private practice might be implemented to ensure a more effective use of scarce medical resources?*

*Should private practice be abolished altogether?*

## 3. Appropriate Health Personnel

The existing formal health services are heavily dependent on the orthodox health workers, doctors and nurses. Most of these are involved for most of their time in curative health care.

**Disruption of rural health facilities by war**

In the provision of health care for Namibian refugees in the Namibian Health and Education Centres, SWAPO has evolved a system emphasising auxiliary health workers such as medical assistants and front-line health workers. The 1980 Country Health Programme has suggested that village health workers should each be trained to cover a population of about 1,000 people.

The experiences of other countries and the experiences of SWAPO in the Health and Education Centres can help in planning how the existing health workers in Namibia may be re-oriented towards the PHC strategy.

Given the size of the population of Namibia it is not possible to justify the establishment of a national medical school. Most Namibian doctors have been trained in South Africa. Consideration of what arrangements might be made with neighbouring countries sympathetic to SWAPO's policies will have to be given. It is essential that such training emphasises the importance of a community health approach as well as clinical competence.

*What types of health personnel will be needed in the formal health services in independent Namibia, and how might their training be organised?*

The crucial contribution of community health workers (CHWs) to the effective provision of PHC is well documented. Selecting acceptable people to be CHWs will depend on the success of popular local involvement in people's control of their health and health care.

There are several policy issues related to community health workers that will benefit from detailed consideration before independence. Namibia's rural population is widely dispersed, and in some areas it may prove difficult to have a single CHW covering 1,000 people's needs. The payment of CHWs has also created problems in some countries' recurrent health budgets.

*What arrangements can be made to provide community health workers for people living in the sparsely populated areas of Namibia?*

*What forms of payment for CHWs in Namibia are locally appropriate and feasible?*

Traditional healers and midwives provide the most accessible care for many rural communities. Their practice is often helpful, sometimes unhelpful but harmless, and sometimes actually does harm.

*Should there be training schemes (e.g. in hygiene) for traditional midwives?*

*How would such training be organised in the more dispersed populations?*

*What are the attitudes of other health workers to these traditional practitioners?*

As part of the independence war SWAPO has trained numbers of paramedical staff. These will be very important as a source of potential health workers in post-independence Namibia. Understandably, they have focussed in their training on first aid and curative care.

*What can ensure that the paramedical staff are effectively incorporated into the health services of Namibia, and can receive additional training in promotive and preventive health care?*

## 4. Health Care for Special Groups

A regrettable and tragic consequence of armed struggle is that many people, combatants and civilians, are injured and disabled. Many such people are young and have made great personal sacrifices besides suffering terrible injuries. Rehabilitative services will be a high priority for Namibia.

*How might services be organised to ensure that such people are adequately cared for and integrated into the community?*

*Besides the people needing rehabilitation services there are other groups such as the elderly and the mentally disabled: How are disabled people to be represented at national level? And at local level? Are there traditional beliefs about the causes of infirmity and disability that need to be considered?*

## 5.  Organising Services to Support Primary Health Care

PHC can improve health if it is planned and implemented in a co-ordinated fashion with actions at various levels – i.e. both in communities and at district and provincial levels – and with a substantial degree of financial autonomy to be able to respond to local needs. On the other hand, there are actions which are most efficiently undertaken at a central government level. These include strategic planning and decisions relating to standardising management and co-ordinating referral systems. Central planning is particularly important in the provision of appropriate pharmaceuticals, transport facilities, specialised medical skills and some administrative support.

*How might essential drugs programmes for different levels of health care be developed?*

*Can schemes for treating common diseases be designed to ensure uniformity?*

*How might a national programme such as a country-wide immunisation project be organised to be sure of involving local representative bodies – and ensuring that such bodies are more than mere implementers of a central plan?*

Any proposals to limit spending on central urban services in favour of expanding rural services are likely to be resisted by those with vested interests to retain and increase central service expenditure. These vested interests include health professionals and the high technology equipment and drug suppliers, as well as the urban elite who expect the most expensive of services to be available to them.

*How can disadvantaged people compete for resources against such powerful interests?*

*Can the redistribution of resources be strengthened by being enshrined in law: e.g. legislation to establish a national health service for all; legal limitations and controls put on private practitioners and medical suppliers; regulations bonding trainee health workers to government services?*

★     ★     ★     ★     ★

This short section has attempted to highlight some of the issues likely to be crucial for a successful re-organisation of the health service in independent Namibia.

In the next five sections we will look briefly at some specific areas of Primary Health Care in rural areas.

## PART TWO: Water and Sanitation

In Chapter 4 we discussed the major patterns of disease in underdeveloped countries. We showed how poor water supply and poor sanitation facilities, along with poor nutrition, are the most frequent associates of the common diseases. These water-borne, water-washed and water-related diseases (see Table 2 in Chapter 4) are largely preventable through the implementation of a comprehensive water and sanitation development programme.

It is estimated that over 1.3 billion people in developing countries, most of them in rural areas, are without reasonable access to safe and copious supplies of water, and over 1.7 billion people are without adequate sanitation. Namibia is no exception. There is a plentiful supply of good quality water for the better off residents of the main towns and large farms, but poorer facilities in the urban townships and few or no facilities for the rest of the rural population. Four standards of water are used in Namibia: Class A conforms to the World Health Organisation recommended standard of purity and is provided in much of the urban areas by the Department of Water Affairs: Class B, of lower quality but still suitable for human consumption, is provided in other urban areas; Class C is of poor quality and found in most rural areas; and Class D, recommended only for cattle consumption, is the only water in many remote rural areas.

The quantity of water is a problem in some parts of the towns, and is a major problem in rural areas where water supplies are very sparse and inaccessible.

There is a water-borne sewerage system in the urban areas. In contrast there are virtually no sanitation facilities in the rural areas. Faecal contamination of swamp water in the rainy season is a serious problem.

Water supply and sanitation schemes are introduced by governments because of the expected health benefits. These health benefits are not always the first reason given by communities for better facilities. More often the priority reason is the saving of time and effort needed to fetch and carry water which is the most easily felt (and measured) benefit. Women in particular often spend several hours each day fetching enough water to keep a household going. Sanitation, in contrast, is relatively low on the list of priorities, especially in rural areas.

It follows that the introduction of water and sanitation schemes needs to be handled with some consideration for locally felt needs. Local discussions may be helped by well-distributed information on the relationships between water and disease, and especially the relationships between excreta disposal and disease. This information would need to be set in the context of local communities' current practices for getting and using water, and for excretion.

At the same time, it may also be recognised that the benefits of water and sanitation schemes would extend far beyond health improvements. Time and energy saved in fetching water can be turned to other productive purposes, including income-earning projects. Water itself is not only used for drinking, washing and cooking, but also benefits draught animals and can be used on vegetable gardens. There could therefore be a direct impact on food production, including production for sale. Water is also used in construction, so better housing and storage facilities might also be seen as a result of a water development programme. Not only health but many aspects of living and working conditions and economic development may show improvement.

Resources for water and sanitation development may compete with other urgent budget demands and it may be necessary to argue the case for the widespread benefits beyond improvements in health, and so recruit other ministries into a water campaign. A health ministry may find itself participating alongside rural development and local authority ministries, water supply authorities, agriculture and food ministries and agricultural extension bodies, construction and housing departments, urban and industrial planning bodies as well as the economic planning ministry. This is fairly formidable and can become even more complicated with the involvement of the various international agencies and aid organisations, with their preconceptions and ready-made programmes. A single body might be needed to co-ordinate the programmes, respond to local initiatives and stimulate local participation.

Experiences in other developing countries have shown that Water Affairs engineers tend to promote inappropriate and over-technical solutions. (In Zimbabwe, for example, it was argued by water supply officials that full WHO-standard water, supplied to every household through reticulated piped systems, was essential – 'nothing less' – but when the sums were done it was found that the scheme would cost more than Zimbabwe's entire Gross National Product to install, and more than a third of the GNP each year to run.) A ministry of local government might be in a better position to co-ordinate with the various sectors and facilitate a decentralised, appropriate-technology approach. Local women's groups, schools and church bodies might usefully help to motivate and organise participative water and sanitation projects.

The high density urban townships are a relatively easy target for starting water and sanitation developments and it may be tempting to focus on these areas when considering development strategies. The majority of people, however, living in the rural areas, are suffering the greatest consequences of the lack of resources at present. Any improvements in the urban areas would be expensive, but in the rural areas, with the use of appropriate technology, great benefits can be obtained at a relatively low cost per person.

Many water and sanitation programmes have failed due to problems in maintaining equipment. Developing countries throughout the world have large numbers of broken down or faulty water supplies, and in some countries the rate of breakdown approaches the rate of construction. Operating a completed scheme, and ensuring that it is adequately maintained is most often the area where problems arise. If the scheme has used relatively complicated technology and was built by a non-local construction agency, then the subsequent running and repairing of the equipment will need a trained, skilled labour force available locally, as well as back-up training institutions, spare-parts suppliors and distributers and storage facilities. The costs of operating sophisticated facilities can soon add up to more than the initial construction costs, high as those may have been.

Even where appropriate technology is used, a country-wide programme will be expensive and may look to foreign aid agencies for assistance: the multilateral (such as WHO, UNICEF), bilateral (government-to-government) and non-governmental (church, charity and other voluntary) agencies. These agencies usually prefer to fund the construction and equipping of facilities and expect the recipients to be responsible for running and repairing them. Donor agencies, especially donor governments, may also require that a large part of the funds they donate should be spent on specified equipment and personnel, usually from the donor country. This can make the maintenance and repair problems even worse, particularly if a large number of different agencies have been involved. A useful precaution is for the co-ordinating authority in the recipient country to specify a limited range of equipment and techniques which they are prepared to accept. Where this has been tried in developing countries it has been found that donor agencies are usually prepared to change their approach and conform to the limitations.

One of the major successes in Zimbabwe's water and sanitation development programmes has been the introduction of locally-designed water pumps and pit latrines.* They are cheap to manufacture in kit form and

---

* Details of the Blair Pump and the Ventilated Improved Privy can be obtained from the Blair Laboratories, North Avenue, Harare, Zimbabwe.

**In urban areas water supplies are inadequate**

involve simple, locally-available technology and materials. They use local labour to make and install and can save considerably on foreign currency and foreign expertise. Their practical use in rural schemes can now be demonstrated in Zimbabwe, although a key factor in their successful introduction has been the involvement of the local community, especially women, from the early stages. Liaison with the Blair Institute in Zimbabwe might well benefit the newly independent Namibia.

Water and sanitation schemes are part of rural development generally – an essential part – and like other aspects of development they are of value to a local community as far as that community is prepared for them, wants them, and will use and be responsible for them. Local communities need to be involved in planning and developing their schemes from the earliest stages, and to make decisions about the technology needed in relation to their needs and their ability to run the finished scheme. A series of protected wells, for instance, may be preferable to a borehole and diesel pump which, when not working, is useless.

Special efforts need to be made to educate adults and children alike on the hygienic value of building and using sanitation facilities. Constructing wells and latrines for a local school might be a useful focus to start a community programme, while at the same time promoting hygiene education and construction practice in the school curriculum.

# PART THREE: Maternal and Child Health

In Chapter 3 we discussed the role of women and women's importance in providing health for themselves and their families, as well as women's predominance in the nursing and caring services. We also considered women's social status, and how women's involvement in health care projects was inseparable from involvement generally in all decisions affecting day-to-day living – including explicitly political decisions. In this section we will look briefly at one specific area of women's health: maternal health, and the corollary of maternal health: the health of young children.

Taken together, women of child-bearing age plus children under the age of five constitute nearly half the population of most underdeveloped countries, and Namibia is unlikely to be an exception. Maternal and child health (MCH) is usually viewed as a priority service in such countries: the World Health Organisation states that MCH services are a priority within any health service – mothers and children are the most vulnerable sector of the community and their deaths epitomise the gaps between rich and poor. For a country to develop, its population must be healthy and energetic, which cannot come from an unhealthy childhood and tired mothers.

The priorities for developing an MCH programme need to be based on the most urgent health problems prevailing in Namibia. Is an oral rehydration programme more urgent than an immunisation programme? Is hygiene education more urgent than family planning education? Can these alternative priorities be linked together and developed simultaneously? How can the formal maternity services be linked in with traditional midwives (who might be responsible for as many as 80% or 90% of rural births), and is this desirable?

In the next section on nutrition and underdevelopment we discuss a project in Zimbabwe in which the distribution of food to malnourished young children was linked to health education and local control of the programme. It has also stimulated some mothers to start co-operative agricultural schemes, with advice from local agricultural extension officers. Widespread use was made of the Road to Health card and it introduced the mothers to the value of regular weighing of their childen. Locally available foods were used for the children's feeding, and these were made into meals communally by the mothers – so they quickly saw there were no 'magic' or 'medical' ingredients that led to their child's growth. Thus the supplementary feeding scheme not only distributed food to malnourished children, but had a variety of useful health education and self-help benefits.

A project such as this contrasts with some aid agency programmes that deliver surplus European and American products, including foods such as butter oil and soya flour, and contraceptive pills and devices, with no attempt to educate the recipients about the usefulness (or otherwise) of the aid being given and no attempt to develop local alternatives when the aid is withdrawn. Worse still are the promoters of commercial baby foods and baby milk formula, often using staff dressed as health workers, and who attempt to persuade the mother to use more expensive and usually less healthy alternatives to the child's original diet. Mozambique has banned such infant formula products apart from permitting one supplier to provide goods direct to the government.

Zimbabwe began by announcing that it would take a strong line against commercial producers (principally a subsidiary of Nestles) and produced a booklet for distribution to all health workers which criticised the promotion of baby foods. However, the milk powders remain commercially available and widely distributed in Zimbabwe (possibly because the product is largely constituted from ingredients supplied by the powerful parastatal Zimbabwe Dairy Marketing Board).

When planning services, it is important to bear in mind the vast size of Namibia, and the widespread dispersal of the population. There are enormous difficulties of communication and transport, and in the provision of supplies and other forms of support, which can be exacerbated during the rainy season in some areas, where whole districts may be effectively isolated. Special provision has to be made to ensure that every health care facility is as self-sufficient as possible and that it can provide effective services for as long a period as possible without needing external support.

## Traditional Midwives

One means of utilising scarce resources in remote areas – indeed, any area – is to integrate the formal service with the traditional, local services, so that the two branches of health care support each other instead of developing separately. In Zimbabwe it is estimated that over three-quarters of all births take place at home attended by Traditional Birth Attendants, and it will be impossible to develop the formal maternity services to have all deliveries in health centres or hospitals for the foreseeable future (even assuming it is desirable to try and do this). Traditional Birth Attendants are to be incorporated – or rather 'articulated' – into the formal services. (In Zimbabwe the term Traditional Midwives is preferred, as their role extends far beyond attendance at the birth but includes concern for the child's well-being as the child grows.)

In countries where a single village midwife may serve several dozen

**Monitoring the nutritional status of children**

families it may be feasible to send around a well-equipped mobile training facility to upgrade the traditional practitioners to an acceptable level, and keep them provided with delivery equipment. In Zimbabwe it was considered that such a scheme was not feasible: most Zimbabweans in the rural areas live in smaller, family compounds rather than villages, and they are widely scattered on the available land, so that instead of a single midwife serving a few dozen families there were dozens of midwives serving only a few families each – with each midwife attending only a few births each year. Also, the scheme would cost a lot and depended on bringing in outside training facilities, leaving the local health centres uninvolved. The alternative approach being adopted in the province of Manicaland, as a prototype for other provinces, is for the local health centres to organise a series of training meetings (six to ten), each one to be held when the midwives are able to come to the centre (e.g. once a fortnight), at which discussions and lessons on antenatal, birth, postnatal and immunisation topics are held, and the practical work of the clinic – including the labour ward and the well-baby sessions – are demonstrated. In this way good relations and mutual respect between the formal and the traditional services can be built up. One further point to note is that, instead of giving the midwives sets of equipment for deliveries, a simpler, very cheap 'cord' kit has been developed (string, sterile razor blade, surgical spirit and cotton wool) which is given to each mother attending antenatal clinic. This encourages mothers' attendance and continued liaison with the clinic.

The midwife's concern for the children she delivers continues throughout their childhood – they are her 'cousins'. The midwife is in a key position to be a community MCH worker, promoting both the mothers' and the children's health. She can be involved in encouraging attendance at well-mothers and well-child clinics, immunisation programmes and even nutrition projects. She performs her duties without payment from the national service, although her training costs and the mothers' cord kits are provided from health service funds. She works only infrequently as a midwife and is otherwise a normally-productive member of her community. She is of course answerable to her community through its own normal social relationships and responsibilities. The role of an upgraded midwife can serve as a simple model for the introduction of community health workers, of the sort we have discussed in Chapters 4 and 5.

★     ★     ★     ★     ★

In Namibia, women and children rely greatly on their own resources, their communities' resources and the traditional practitioners for promoting their own health. Introducing and extending the formal health service needs to be organised in a way which involves women and uses the strengths and abilities already existing in the community.

## PART FOUR: Nutrition and underdevelopment

The dramatic diseases of famine – kwashiorkor and marasmus – serious though they are represent only a small proportion of the large number of people, mostly children, who are chronically malnourished. One recent report estimated that nine out of every ten children in the Southern African region suffer from some form of malnourishment.[1]

Not only do these children show slow and stunted growth but they are also highly susceptible to infectious diseases. Ailments which might be only a minor problem for a well-fed child, such as measles or diarrhoea, become major crises in a chronically under-fed child, and are often fatal. The diseases in turn may reduce the child's appetite and ability to absorb food, further weakening the child.

One of the most insidious consequences of undernutrition is that the child may fail to reach his or her full intellectual potential. Poor nutrition in the first three years of life results in impaired brain growth, and in older children is associated with decreased physical activity and exploration, essential for intellectual development.

Undernutrition is primarily due to a general food and energy deficiency. In underdeveloped countries the staple food is usually bulky and children may find it difficult to eat enough of this staple to satisfy their energy (calorie) needs, particularly if their opportunities to eat are restricted to less than three meals each day.

There are two direct interventions that can be made to improve food and calorie intake. One is to increase the frequency of meals and the other is to supplement the bulky staple with high-energy foods such as those containing fats and oils.

Before considering intervention strategies, though, it is useful to ask what leads to undernutrition. Simple lack of food is the most important factor in childhood undernutrition – protein deficiency has been shown to be secondary to straightforward lack of calories. Seasonal changes in the numbers of malnourished children is a well-recognised phenomenon and is related to the marginality of food supplies in 'subsistence' economies, where food from the previous harvest may run out while the next season's crops are still growing. That the supplies of food should be so near the borderline emphasises the relationship between malnutrition and the quality of the land: poor nutrition is inseparable from the distribution of land and from its quality, and so is inseparable from colonialism and the process of underdevelopment.

The example of Zimbabwe can be taken to illustrate some of the ways in which colonial underdevelopment adversely affects nutrition. The legacy of food shortages and undernutrition inherited at independence and some of the interventions introduced after 1980 will be discussed.

## Undernutrition in Zimbabwe: The Colonial Legacy

Prior to Zimbabwe's independence in April 1980 the amount of undernutrition among the population was unknown. Figures available indicate that it was high – in some rural areas there were reports of 80% of the children being affected. The highest levels were reported among the children of the black farmworkers on white-owned commercial farms, where wages were low and food 'rations' meagre and insufficient for the workers' families.

In the rest of rural Zimbabwe, where four fifths of the population live, the food problem was mainly a consequence of the land distribution that was imposed under colonialism. Through a series of Land Tenure Acts the most fertile parts of the country were designated as 'European' areas and the vast majority of Zimbabweans were forced to live in so-called African reserves or 'Tribal Trust Lands' (TTLs). These areas had the poorest soil, the lowest rainfall, the highest risk of erosion and the highest incidence of endemic diseases. The land became increasingly unproductive over the years while the population continued to expand. By 1980 land was occupied by blacks and whites in the ratio 50:50, while the rural population was in the ratio 100:1.

The land problem was compounded by the inequitable distribution of resources. The commercial farm owners enjoyed the benefit of a complex support structure which included credit facilities, agricultural technology and training, as well as transport and storage networks and distribution outlets, largely denied to the peasant farmers in the TTLs. The myth developed that the high productivity of the commercial farms was something intrinsic and relied on being run by whites, a myth which persists today and which overlooks the extensive infrastructural support and capital investment which are the real bases for farming productivity.

Colonialism also adversely affected the people's eating habits in a number of ways. Groundnuts, which are high in energy and thus particularly nutritious for children, were traditionally an important component of the diet. They were ground into a form of peanut butter to supplement the staple food. It was often added to young children's porridge, and added to the vegetable, bean or meat 'relish' or sauce which accompanied the meals of the older children and adults. Groundnuts themselves were also used as snacks by the older children.

By 1980 groundnuts were used sparingly or not at all, since under the colonial pricing system they had become an important cash crop, grown for sale rather than for eating.

Not only were groundnuts used less in the diet, but the money obtained by selling them was used to purchase less nutritious food such as tea, sugar and white bread. This can be partly attributed to commercial factors such as advertising and the controlled distribution to rural shops, and partly to the effects of colonialism in undermining people's traditional values so that they aspire to the values and ways of the colonial power.

The change of feeding practices in children was further reinforced by health workers and nutritionists who, in accordance with the prevailing medical beliefs, taught that protein was the missing component in children's diet. Health education posters in every hospital and clinic condemned the use of maize meal and advocated in its place dairy products, fish and even liver – foods which were expensive, difficult to find and, as it now turns out, largely unnecessary.

The migration of men to the towns and industries to earn money led to great burdens being placed on the women who remained in the rural areas. With their many responsibilities for growing food, collecting water and firewood, caring for the children, the elderly and the sick in the extended family group, it became difficult for them to find enough time to ensure that their youngest children were having meals cooked and fed to them frequently enough.

The chronic food problems were greatly exacerbated by the Rhodesian military. The policy of forcing people into overcrowded 'protected villages' often many miles from their farmland, and the imposition of curfews, meant many peasants found it impossible to cultivate their land or tend their cattle, many of which died. Not only was food production under these circumstances seriously hampered but the Rhodesian forces, under the codename 'Operation Turkey', actually destroyed people's food stocks if they considered it might reach the liberation fighters. Finally, as the war years drew to a close, many areas of the country experienced two consecutive years of drought, and were in desperate need of assistance at the time of independence.

## Food Programmes in Newly-Independent Zimbabwe

### A.   *United Nations Food Programmes*

The food shortage and the return to Zimbabwe of large numbers of refugees prompted a massive food relief programme which continued from early 1980 until May 1981. Funded by the United Nations High Commission for Refugees (UNHCR), it was initially administered by local voluntary agencies and subsequently by the Zimbabwe Government Department of Social Services.

People received food on the basis of stated need, whether or not they had been refugees. The programme was very successful. At its peak, food was being distributed to 800,000 people. Wastage and theft were low although some people with adequate food stocks claimed food relief as a reward for their part in the liberation struggle.

Probably the biggest problem was that some of the people who were in most need of food relief did not receive it because they lived in remote border areas which could not be reached by the programme's vehicles. Very little high energy food was provided and so the programme was of limited value to young children.

The UNHCR also funded an 'agricultural pack' of implements, winter vegetable and maize seeds, and these were widely distributed to refugees and peasant farmers. Delays in distribution, lack of extension staff and drought prevented the full benefit of this scheme being realised.

### B.   *The Children's Supplementary Feeding Programme (CSFP)*

Nutrition surveys carried out in rural areas immediately after independence showed a high prevalence of undernutrition, especially among one- to five-year-old children. In some districts 70% of these children were found to be undernourished. It was clear that these children's health would deteriorate before the next harvest could be gathered and that from late 1980 until April 1981 would be a crisis period. A Children's Supplementary Feeding Programme (CSFP) was planned as a relief exercise, but with a nutrition education component.

The initiative was taken by a number of local and external voluntary agencies in co-operation with the Ministry of Health, and it was funded by the agencies. One- to five-year-old children in rural areas were selected as the target group and a measurement of the mid upper arm circumference was used as a simple way of identifying undernourished children in this age range. A circumference of less than 13 cm led to a child's admission into the programme.

Much thought was given to establishing the best way to improve these children's health. A supplementary meal was chosen to be an addition to, and not a substitute for, their normal diets, and locally-grown foods were considered more appropriate than imported ones. Hence a dish of maize meal, together with beans, groundnuts and vegetable oil, was designed to provide each child with at least an extra third of their daily requirements.

The organisation of the CSFP within each district depended on the motivated people and the material resources available in each area. The political structures that had developed during the war were involved in organising the CSFP at all levels from district to village, and they were crucial in planning, starting and running the programme. The network included school teachers, health workers, community workers, party representatives, and above all the mothers themselves.

Feeding points were established near to people's homes and fields so that children could attend easily. Each point had a locally-selected supervisor who kept a daily register and supervised the cooking of the meals, which was done by the mothers in a rota. The first feeding points opened in January 1981 and by three months were operating all over the country. At the peak of the programme nearly 100,000 children were receiving meals.

Various delays meant that feeding began later than anticipated, but it was becoming clear that the harvest was likely to be poor following another drought in many parts of the country. As the programme continued, greater emphasis was placed on nutrition education. A poster was produced emphasising the importance of high-energy foods and this was widely distributed. At many feeding points other health initiatives were introduced, such as the use of the Road to Health (Growth) Charts and oral rehydration for the treatment of diarrhoea. An evaluation of the CSFP carried out in 1981[2] showed that it had largely succeeded in its aims. The evaluation was designed after the programme had started, leading to some problems getting adequate objective figures comparing CSFP children with a control group. The figures available showed that the children in the programme gained a considerable amount of weight and that this was attributable to the programme itself. Responses to a questionnaire of the mothers showed that mothers recognised the improvement in their children's health and that in many areas the educational message had been accepted.

## C.  The Communal Groundnut Production Project

People in some districts where the CSFP had been particularly successful and well-organised made a request for assistance to develop communal production plots of groundnuts and maize. They wanted to turn their feeding points into children's play-centres and provide some extra food to all the children attending there. Funding for 40 production plots was given by a voluntary agency.

The Ministry of Health subsequently adopted the idea and in each province 100 communities, selected on strict criteria through the CSFP, were provided with enough groundnut seeds, gypsum and fertiliser to cultivate half a hectare. The programme was greeted with much enthusiasm and has involved close liaison between health workers, agricultural extension workers, women from the Ministry of Women's Affairs and Community Development and the communities themselves. Only the continuing drought has hampered its success.

**Conclusion**

Undernutrition is still a problem in Zimbabwe. Four consecutive years of drought have had serious effects on food production and on the programmes aimed at assisting development. Yet drought itself is not an explanation for undernutrition. In Zimbabwe today food is being exported to other countries. The distribution of land and resoureces remains essentially the same as it was at Independence. Land Resettlement Programmes have been modest and slow, the economic infrastructure still favours the large commercial farms, and many of the subsidy and pricing schemes which influence cash-cropping remain.

Nutrition education is obviously important, but its impact is limited by other factors. Many women know that their children need frequent meals but simply do not have the time to prepare them. They may wish to grow groundnuts for their children, but must first find the money to pay for the seeds and the fertiliser. Health education is usually directed towards women – the mothers – yet it is usually the men who make the financial decisions and decide what crops are grown and how much is sold for cash.

One of the most important aspects of the CSFP was the involvement of local political structures, and the programme was most successful where these structures were well-organised. In turn, the CSFP helped to give substance and credibility to the newly-formed representative bodies in the post-Independence period.

A most important feature has been the part played by women – the health workers, community workers, teachers, feeding point supervisors, and particularly the mothers themselves. Although both men and women took part in decision making it was onto the already overburdened women that the extra work of the programme fell. This raises questions about how such programmes use women, and what women gain from participating. Involvement *can* help women gain self-confidence, knowledge and organising skills that are essential if they are to take control of their own development.

# PART FIVE: Oral Health

We will start this section by putting Oral Health – often called Dental Health – in its wider social setting. Like our general health, our oral health is intimately bound up with the way we live. To illustrate dental health in its social context we will begin with a story – the story of Maria, a ten-year-old child. It is told by a dentist who worked as a *co-operante* in the People's Republic of Mozambique in 1977.

I first met Maria when she was brought to the Central Hospital in Maputo. She was small, she was sick and she was frightened. My Portuguese was adequate to communicate simply, but she did not speak Portuguese. She sat in the dental chair, her head hardly reaching the headrest behind her. Her face was swollen on both sides and she had pus dribbling from sores beneath her chin. When she opened her mouth I could see the stumps of only a few of her lower teeth. Radiographs showed the bone of her lower jaw to have been eaten away by infection. She had osteomyelitis of the mandible, a chronic destructive infection of her lower jaw. Sadly this is a fairly common condition in many underdeveloped countries. She was put on high doses of antibiotics and with simple curettage the infections were controlled and her mouth healed, leaving her without any lower teeth. I was able to make a simple denture for her, which at least would see her through to young adulthood before it would need replacing.

To set Maria's condition in context we must learn something of her history. She had been born the first of ten children to a family in a small village in the northern-most province of Mozambique, Cabo Delgado. Three years after she was born she and her family were moved to a 'protected village' by the Portuguese colonial power.

There was a nightly curfew and the 'village' was more like a prison. Maria's mother had to rise very early in the morning to go and fetch water and work in the fields. Whilst Maria was an only child there was little problem, but as the other children were born the work increased. The extended family members couldn't offer much help because they too faced the same hardships. Her father was contracted to work in a large kapok plantation a long way distant although still in the same province. He was able to earn some money but only a small amount.

On occasions Maria visited Montepuez, the nearest small town. When she did, she was struck by the fact that when she stood in front of the few shops her nose just reached above the windowsill, while the children of the Portuguese settlers of her age were way above the same height. She also realised she could not read the signs or the prices of the goods in the shops. And anyway, she had no money.

At Independence, Maria's family felt relief. The curfew was lifted, Maria and her brothers and sisters could attend the newly-opened school in the village and her father was able to send them more money. The visits to Montepuez became more frequent and included the purchase of sweets and the fizzy drink Fanta.

One day Maria awoke with extremely bad toothache and had the day off school. The toothache continued and various family remedies were tried. None of these seemed successful so Maria was taken by her mother to the local *currendeiro* (traditional healer). After a long discussion with Maria's mother he produced from a dried milk tin some twigs and made a fire. With a bamboo pipe he blew the smoke at Maria's swollen face for some minutes. As the *currendeiro* explained, the idea was to kill the little worm which was destroying Maria's teeth. Certainly the pain subsided although the swelling remained. Maria went back to school and continued life as before.

Some months later the swelling and the pain increased again until one night the abscess burst and pus began to trickle down Maria's neck. In the morning Maria's mother was considerably alarmed by Maria's appearance. They hurried to Montepuez to visit the local hospital. There they met Jorge, a newly-trained *Agente de Odontoestomatologia* (Dental Hygienist and Emergency Dresser). Jorge prescribed a series of antibiotic injections for the next five days. As he prepared to give the first injection he warned Maria that unfortunately he only had three hyperdermic needles and they were getting a little blunt. He was as gentle as possible but nonetheless Maria found the experience quite painful. The next day she knew what to expect and was more tense and the injection felt even more painful. The same was repeated on the third day and this time, unfortunately, Maria was in tears. By the morning of the fourth day she was feeling better and persuaded her mother that she need not see Jorge again and could return to school. Maria never completed the series of injections. Her face healed and she forgot about her problems until a few months later.

This time she was in serious trouble when she awoke with a very swollen face and extremely intense pain and obviously had a fever. They returned to Jorge immediately but unfortunately Jorge could no longer provide them with antibiotics as the hospital had run out. He suggested they should go to the provincial hospital in Pemba. Travelling on the extremely overcrowded bus, Maria and her mother arrived in Pemba. Eventually they were seen by a kind Mozambican woman doctor who took one look at Maria and suggested that she should be admitted to the hospital immediately. For the first time Maria was separated from her mother and slept in a bed with sheets on it. Naturally she found this very frightening. After some time on the limited antibiotic supplies that the hospital had, Maria was no better. She was therefore flown to Maputo where it was believed there would be more help available. She had to fly as there was no road or railway going directly North to South. All the roads and railways came East-wards from the interior of Africa because they had been constructed during colonial times to carry raw materials and agricultural produce to the coast for shipment to Europe.

This story is told to illustrate how dental health is influenced by social, economic and political forces. In planning oral health services it is important to consider how these social factor influence oral health, as they do every other aspect of health.

Let us analyse a little more the factors which led Maria to Maputo for treatment. First, she was born at a time of acute crisis in the struggle for the liberation of her country, and her family was forced into the so-called protected village, disrupting normal agricultural production and social relations. Her father was forced to seek employment a long distance from home. The burden of providing for a large family had fallen almost entirely on Maria's mother. Not surprisingly, under these conditions the family diet deteriorated resulting in chronic undernutrition for Maria, her mother and her brothers and sisters. The changes in the diet after independence, allowing so-called luxury items to be available to Maria, was irresistible. Her consumption of sugar increased dramatically, leading to dental decay. Her visits to the traditional healer had not resulted in long-lasting improvements in health – although many traditional ideas could be incorporated into oral health services. Her delay in obtaining antibiotic injections and the inadequacy of that treatment due to the deficiencies in both equipment and materials had allowed her condition to deteriorate even further. This deterioration was worse because of Maria's chronic undernourishment.

**Planning for Oral Health**

The development of oral health services will depend on two principal factors:

1. The ability to analyse the existing problems and the resources available to combat those problems;
2. The ability to mobilise *all* available resources to maintain, promote and attain oral health.

### A.  The Analysis of the Problem

Problems of oral health can best be analysed using simple epidemiological methods. There are a number of excellent World Health Organisation publications which give details of such methods (see the Appendix).

The three principal dental diseases are: Dental Caries, Periodontal Disease and Oral Malignancies. Once the prevalence of these conditions has been established for different age groups within the population, an attempt can be made to assess trends that have been occurring in the past few years and which are likely to occur immediately following independence. With respect to dental caries the chances of sugar suddenly becoming more available is important to assess.

### B.  The Analysis of Available Resources

This analysis includes looking at the available trained health workers for oral health: Dentists, Dental Assistants, Doctors, Nurses, Teachers, and Traditional Healers.

A Primary Health Care approach is based upon mobilising the mass of the people to protect and promote their own health. So *dental health education* must form the basis of any programme for oral health. Who influences the behaviour of mothers and primary school children? What public health measures are available to protect and promote oral health?

Not only must resources be considered in terms of people and techniques but also in terms of equipment and materials. It is very hard to relieve dental pain without a minimum of equipment and materials. Any programme must set certain priorities. The first of these might be the provision and development of emergency oral health services. The second priority might be the development of a preventive programme linked to general health promotion and prevention programmes.

### C.  The Mobilisation of Available Resources

Essentially this is a political activity. If it is decided that health is the right of all people, then this must include and not exclude their mouths. Oral health programmes need to be included in general health programmes. As we saw in the story of Maria, it is clear that many of the factors such as poor hygiene and poor nutrition which lead to general ill-health also lead to oral ill-health. Mobilising resources needs to be co-ordinated, and we discuss the development of a coherent plan in the next section.

## Planning Oral Health Services

The planning of oral health services has a number of stages which we show in the diagram on the next page. These stages can be identified as forming two cycles. One is concerned with the actual planning, implementation and evaluation of oral health services and the second is concerned with the planning, development, implementation and evaluation of training programmes for appropriate oral health workers. The two can proceed hand in hand.

The 'information' shown in the diagram is the result of the analysis described earlier. The strategies selected to solve the problems will depend on the pattern of oral health found at independence. The planning process assumes a good knowledge of the effectiveness and efficiency of different methods of tackling oral disease. Much information is available but little has yet been produced under the circumstances of poor underdeveloped countries. So it is important to choose strategies with caution and with the proviso that the methods being tried have not been evaluated under the prevailing circumstances. This highlights the need to include in any oral health plan a small evaluation unit to monitor the progress of oral health programmes. Methods of evaluation and re-planning need to be built in from the start.

The planning cycle underlines the need to develop specific legislation relating to the development of oral health services. This should not, of course, be the restrictive forms of legislation that exist in most capitalist countries and which serve the needs of the professionals rather than those of the people.

## Oral Health Training Programmes

The oral health goals and strategies for achieving these goals directly affect the types of training programmes to be developed. An early priority would be to develop *task lists* of the jobs that have to be performed, and then divide the list up into *job descriptions*. Hence the number of different types of oral health workers can be determined. Where personnel with adequate educational levels are not available it may not be appropriate to have many levels

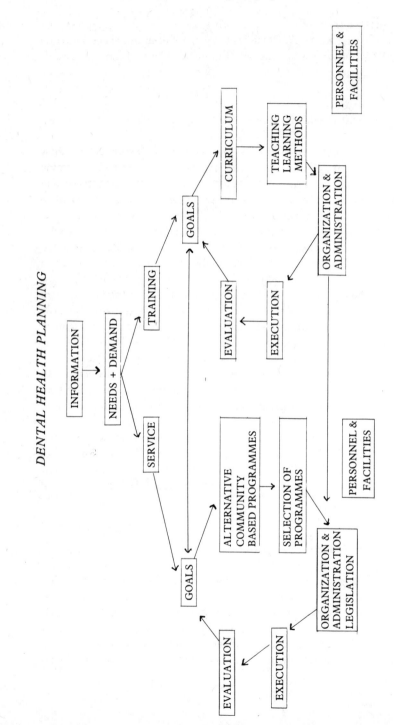

DENTAL HEALTH PLANNING

of health worker. Primary oral health care can be provided by people with very little formal education.

Having decided what types of worker are to be trained, curricula may need to be developed for each of them, with appropriate methods of evaluating the curricula at the end of the courses and a further evaluation of the whole programme and its effect on oral health carried out later. The results can then be measured against the original goals set, and adjustments can be made to ensure that those goals are being achieved.

Table 1 summarises the types of oral health worker in Mozambique. For these different levels of worker, job descriptions were developed and curricula written for the first two types of clinical personnel: the *agente* and the *auxiliar*.

*Table 1: Categories of Oral Health Worker in Mozambique*

| Grade | Oral Health Category of worker | Dental Laboratory Category of worker |
|---|---|---|
| I | Dentist (Medico-Odontoestomatologista) | – |
| II | Dental Technician (Technico-Odontoesto-matologista) | Dental Laboratory Technician (Technico do Laboratorio Dental) |
| III | Dental Hygienist/ Emergency Dresser (Agente-Odontoestom-tologista) | Laboratory Officer (Agente do Laboratorio Dental) |
| IV | Dental Assistant (Auxiliar-Odontoesto-matologista) | Laboratory Assistant (Auxilio do Laboratorio Dental) |

Whilst there is a lack of concrete data on oral health in Namibia at present, it is important to develop methods for planning and establishing oral health programmes well in advance so that they can be started as soon after independence as possible. Evidence from Mozambique suggests that changes in the pattern of consumption of sugar occurred almost immediately after independence. The effect is very rapid on the teeth of young children, and once these teeth are decayed they can never be returned to their original state. There will be a legacy of damaged teeth for the rest of the lifetime of that generation. Thought could be given at an early stage to nutrition policy with respect to the use of sugar among other items, sugar being the most important with regard to oral health.

# PART SIX: Rehabilitation Services

There is a widespread belief that 'rehabilitation' is a *good thing* and that it ought to be systematically introduced into all health services. Before supporting the introduction or extension of rehabilitation services, however, it is well to take a critical look at this whole subject. It is particularly important to do this now because 'rehabilitation', like medicine, is being increasingly criticised by the very people who are most supposed to benefit from its practices – disabled people.

## 1.  Chronic Problems in Rehabilitation

Rehabilitation literature, even from its earliest days, has been concerned with several questions which are raised over and over again, and despite the many answers they are *still* being asked.

Although there have been many attempts to define basic terms in the field, such as rehabilitation, disability, etc., no satisfactory agreement has been reached. In particular, why after so long, unlike other branches of medicine where general agreement about terms can usually be expected, is it still so difficult to be precise about what rehabilitation is meant to be and what it is meant to achieve?

Related to the difficulty in defining terms is the difficulty in identifying the appropriate, or basic, discipline that should support rehabilitation practice. Why has it proved to be so difficult for rehabilitation to become a recognised sector within the health service with its own accepted basic discipline behind it? There is confusion and disagreement about which discipline should be dominant in influencing the character of rehabilitation, or even if medicine is an appropriate base from which to develop a rehabilitation service.

Thirdly, how does the service offered in rehabilitation differ from those services offered in any *good* medical practice? It has been argued that the general goals of rehabilitation and all good medicine are the same – i.e. returning the patient to a maximum state of health, to a former job and to a normal way of life wherever possible. If this is so, then the main reason why the concept of rehabilitation was introduced into the health service was because the already existing medical practice was inadequate. Instead of improving the inadequate service, then, the response was to add yet another specialism to the medical service and to leave the inadequate service untouched.

Fourthly, how can the rehabilitation team work more effectively and harmoniously? This question, of course, also covers more sensitive questions about who should chair or co-ordinate the team? Which profession should have the final say in any decisions about an individual's rehabilitation programme and who should have the final legal responsibility for the patient? How can the rivalry between different professional workers, about who does what to the patient, be sorted out?

Since the idea of rehabilitation was first introduced the term has been applied to specialised practices in two quite separate services – medical services and vocational, or employment, services (and some might argue that a new, community or social rehabilitation service is also developing). The question is, what is the difference between medical and vocational rehabilitation and what unites these services under the same name?

Finally, it is being increasingly recognised that the 'normative' goal of rehabilitation (i.e. its aim of trying to make the patient look and behave as normal as possible) can mislead both the professional and the patient about what problem really needs to be solved. It could be argued, for example, that the central problem should be seen as one of trying to make society fit for disabled people rather than trying to fit disabled people into society. Why are the goals set by the rehabilitation professionals not always appropriate when seen through the eyes of disabled people?

The fact that after so many years these questions still trouble the champions of rehabilitation strongly suggests chronic problems in the original concept. This view is supported by criticisms of the rehabilitation services that are coming from the new organisations of disabled people. In general these organisations criticise the rehabilitation services for failing to lead to any substantial improvements in the *social* situation of disabled people despite the earlier hopes when it was first being introduced into the health services. The relative gap between the situation of able-bodied people and disabled people has remained! Disillusion has followed and increasingly led disabled people to the view that they must become directly involved in setting up, staffing and running their own services. The crisis in rehabilitation is deepening.

## 2. Rehabilitation: Adjusting the Limits of Medical Science?

Medicine is basically concerned with curing illness and injury and helping the patient to be as *normal* as possible. Because of its 'normative' assumptions and its focus on the individual, the permanently impaired person continues to be seen as a patient, with a problem, and the search for a cure carries on. When no medicine is found to solve the problem other branches of the profession such as surgery and bio-engineering develop – e.g. retinal surgery to cure blindness, the attachment of artificial joints and limbs to cure motor impairments and the introduction of various transplants to replace tissues and organs.

When, however, the profession has done all it can and a permanent impairment still remains, medicine has little to offer. Faced with this reality, and the pressures of the second world war which demanded something for returning injured soldiers, the medical profession began to look at ways of helping impaired individuals fit into society. This did not mean that the profession began to develop a methodology appropriate to the social problems faced by disabled people. On the contrary, the profession applied its individualistic and 'normative' assumptions (i.e. to fit disabled people into the able-bodied and non-accessible society that was excluding them), and developed a new medicalised approach to social issues – rehabilitation. Thus a social challenge was reinterpreted as a problem falling under the control of, hopefully, the new branch of rehabilitation medicine.

The introduction of rehabilitation broadened the perspective of medical practice with disabled people and community goals were more forcefully encouraged. This, of course, underlines the fact that until then the medical profession had treated disabled people, like most of its patients, largely in isolation of social issues. It is worth noting that had such a social perspective been included in normal medical practice, as it should, then the emergence of a rehabilitation service would have been unlikely! Where medicine is socialised, properly incorporated into a comprehensive health service, and responsive to personal needs and community issues, then it is difficult to imagine a need for a specialised rehabilitation service for disabled people.

Introducing rehabilitation services into an inadequate medical service, however, had a positive effect on the lives of disabled people, at least when it was initially developed. Firstly, at the personal level, a more systematic approach to helping people with injuries and permanent impairments was introduced. This helped disabled people acquire some skills which could be of benefit to them when facing the barriers of an able-bodied designed social and physical environment. There was also the more systematic development of aids and appliances and the growing awareness of the need to adapt patients' homes if disabled people were to move out of the rehabilitation centres. In time these developments meant that more disabled people could function independently in the community and acquire the social and personal experience which enabled them to make a more informed criticism of the health and rehabilitation services. Secondly, at the more social level, it brought the medical profession, and disabled people, into greater contact with an increasing number of different professions and some such professionals, like those in the employment services, had a quite different approach, which in turn helped disabled people better appreciate their situation as a whole. It became increasingly clear that the fundamental problem to be faced by disabled people is the socio-political one – that of struggling to make society fit for all the people who live in it.

The introduction of rehabilitation treatment procedures into the hospital, or special day care centre, was historically important because it influenced people to see permanent impairment as raising social, and not just personal, problems. The need for multi-disiplinary teams demanded a more holistic approach towards the personal and social problems faced by disabled people. Having recognised that the help given to people with permanent impairments was limited by its lack of a social and holistic perspective, a section of the medical profession organised for this gap to be filled. However, instead of pressing for a genuine socialised form of medical practice where the patient and the community are more involved in health issues they attempted the impossible. Under the term 'rehabilitation' they made a medical interpretation of the social problems facing disabled people and then tried to make this the dominant framework for the interventions of a whole team of multidisciplinary workers. Despite good intentions, the attempt of the medical profession to make social judgements about fitting disabled people into an able-bodied world and to systematise this under the umbrella term 'rehabilitation' cannot succeed. Rehabilitation medicine is not the appropriate starting point for assisting disabled people to live in the community. Nor is medicine the appropriate base from which to develop a fuller understanding of the real disability felt by people who have a permanent physical impairment.

## 3. Who Decides What it Means to be Rehabilitated?

Starting from a medical base, with its focus on the individual and its aim of curing problems, rehabilitation moved into the arena of social problems. In doing this it tried to encourage a curative approach to the social problems that disabled people face. When it was possible to fit a disabled person into the able-bodied world then that person was considered to have been rehabilitated. This means, of course, that the person also had to accept a serious limit to what he or she expected to be able to do in the community – e.g. not

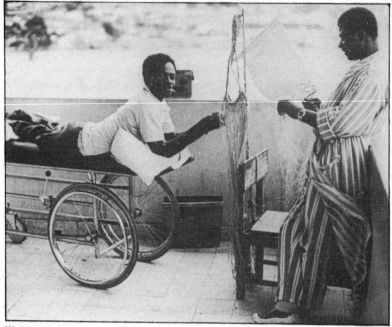

**War wounded**

use public transport, not be considered as a possible marriage partner or wage earner, etc. Rehabilitation professionals, therefore, are also always concerned about helping their patients adjust to their so-called limitations. This is important psychologically because it helps to brainwash disabled people into accepting that the present able-bodied world is the only world that one can fit into.

From this point of view the whole struggle to eliminate the social problems created by an able-bodied designed world, that disabled people are supposed to fit into, is best tackled by the experts who have the right rehabilitation approach – the able-bodied professional with a curative mentality (or even the disabled person if he or she has an able-bodied, or 'normal', and properly adjusted, mentality!) This, of course, means that disabled people are left permanently passive, permanently dependent upon 'expert' others to solve their problems for them and permanently within a limiting able-bodied social and physical environment.

To be a functioning human being within a social world, however, a person must play an active role in influencing the life of the community. For there to be any real advance in the integration of disabled people into society, therefore, it is necessary for disabled people to assert their own interpretation of what the world should be like, in their own interests, and for them to take an active part in actually helping to mould the world according to this viewpoint. This means that disabled people, like any other group who have faced social discrimination, have to organise to have a voice of their own so that their interpretation of the world can be expressed. Such organisations then become the channel for influencing the power structure of society and for communicating with other social groups. It is in this way that disabled people become the active agents of their own rehabilitation into the community. Their organisations become the court of appeal, deciding what is meant by rehabilitation, and the final judge of when disabled people have truly been rehabilitated into the community.

## 4. Rehabilitation, or Integrated Living Services?

When good medical practice is achieved with the active participation of patients and the community then there can be real progress in the elimination of permanent impairment both by prevention (e.g. reducing industrial accidents) and by more effectively utilising social wealth (e.g. spending money on health and related research rather than armaments) to develop surgical interventions, bio-engineering (e.g. regeneration of tissue, organs and limbs), tissue and organ transplants and improved artificial body parts.

The problem of dealing with the social barriers, however, requires the direct involvement of disabled people. With the active support of local communities the representative oranisations of disabled people could be encouraged to set up 'Centres for Integrated Living'. Such centres, run and largely staffed by disabled people, but working closely with health and social welfare professions and representatives of other groups in the community, could concentrate on teaching newly disabled people independence skills, providing information, supervising housing and public building adaptations, ensuring accessible public transport, monitoring the way disability is presented to the public and in schools, and ensuring full employment of disabled people. Integrated Living Centres could become the channel for ensuring that the voice of disabled people is accepted into all the decision-making processes of society. It is in these centres, in particular, that medical and other professionals could become a resource to be used by disabled people. Under these conditions the 'expert' or professional becomes a teacher rather than a therapist or someone who *does* things *to* and *for* disabled people. With the advent of good medical practice and the active involvement of disabled people in social affairs in their own interest the whole need for a rehabilitation medicine then falls away.

# References

1   Report of the *Save the Children Fund (U.K.)*, 1983.
2.  *The Children's Supplementary Feeding Programme in Zimbabwe* report prepared for the Ministry of Health, Zimbabwe, by the voluntry agencies initially sponsoring the programme, Harare, 1982.

# 7

# Urban and Industrial Health

The greater part of disease and death patterns is accounted for by social factors relating to the ownership and control of productive resources. People who are not classified as 'white' run an unevenly high risk of disease, even after taking into account the relatively rare 'genetic influences' which account for 5 percent at most. By far the most important single feature in the 'racially' stratified patterns in Namibia is malnutrition. This is reflected also in high mortality rates, particularly through gastroenteritis and pneumonia.

For the individual worker, shortage of food makes wage employment necessary for survival. So many people are in this position that competition for employment is fierce and consequently wages are low. Low wages, since they barely keep the worker and some of his family alive, prevent people in this position of dependence from getting out of it. Thus the danger of malnutrition is central to the production and maintenance of a cheap labour supply. It is at the heart of disease and death patterns, and indeed the entire social fabric, of contemporary Namibia.

Death rates in Windhoek provide some indications of the relative burden of disease among urban dwellers of different social class. In the Mayoral Report for the City of Windhoek 1981 (presented 15/3/1982), it was claimed that the death rates for whites, coloured and blacks were 6.5, 15.8 and 18.7 per 1,000 people respectively. If the population figures upon which these are based are believed, this means coloureds at all ages are 2.4 times more at risk of dying than are whites, while blacks are 2.9 times more at risk (i.e. approximately 300 percent).

These figures, however, should be viewed with some caution. By claiming that there are more white residents than exist in reality, presumably to mask the exodus of whites, the Administration has produced an untoward 'decline' in mortality by inflating the denominator on which the calculation is based.

Similarly, distortions in the figures among blacks are also likely. Most important among these is that many blacks in Windhoek are young adults, migrants from the rural areas, who are at a lower risk of dying than the resident urban population which contain children and old people. The figures

**South African military presence**

for blacks, although they probably underestimate the actual size of population, therefore actually 'reduce' the crude death rates.

Apart from the biases implicit in crude death rates when the age structures of the populations are different, other biases in the rates for various skin colour groups probably lead to an underestimation of the real differences. Additionally, these data pertain to Windhoek where, bad as things may be for township dwellers, living conditions are considerably better than in the country at large. In the rural areas these crude death rates are likely to be substantially higher, but this is difficult to investigate further in the absence of the most basic registration system for births and deaths. Data from certain rural hospitals allow breakdown by cause of death among all deaths occurring in those hospitals, but it was not possible to link these figures to a defined population (see Table 1).

Data from 12 randomly selected monthly reports of the Medical Officer for Health of the City of Windhoek between 1976 and 1981 demonstrate the 10 main causes of death (Table 1). Perinatal deaths and TB feature more prominantly among coloureds and blacks than among whites. Noteworthy is the fact that heart disease and cancers feature quite highly in all three skin colour categories.

Based on the official population figures for Windhoek for the period

Table 1: Top 10 Killers: Windhoek 1976-1981
(From Reports of the City Medical Office)

| Rank | White | % total deaths | Coloureds | % total deaths |
|---|---|---|---|---|
| 1 | Heart Disease ex IHD | 22% | Perinatal Deaths | 18% |
| 2 | Cancers | 20% | Cancers | 15% |
| 3 | Ischaemic Heart Dis. | 17% | Stroke & Hypertension | 10% |
| 4 | Stroke & Hypertension | 10% | Heart Disease ex IHD | 10% |
| 5 | Motor Accidents | 3% | TB | 8% |
| 6 | All Other Accidents | 3% | Motor Accidents | 8% |
| 7 | Non-infectious diseases of infants | 2% | All other accidents | 7% |
| 8 | Pulmonary Infections | 1% | Ischaemic Heart Disease | 5% |
| 9 | Liver Cirrhosis | 1% | Pulmonary Infections | 3% |
| 10 | Diabetes Melitus | 1% | Gut infections except among neonates | 3% |
| | Black Urban | | Black Rural (Estimate)* | |
| 1 | Cancers | 15% | TB | 17% |
| 2 | Perinatal deaths | 13% | Perinatal Deaths | 13% |
| 2 | TB | 11% | Chest infections | 13% |
| 4 | Chest infections | 11% | Stroke & Hypertension | 7% |
| 5 | Stroke & Hypertension | 7% | All Other Heart Dis. | 6% |
| 6 | Motor Accidents | 7% | Cancers | 6% |
| 7 | Ischaemic Heart Dis. | 6% | Ischaemic Heart Dis. | 6% |
| 8 | Other Heart disease | 5% | Gut Infections except among neonates | 5% |
| 9 | All other accidents | 5% | All Other Accidents | 4% |
| 10 | Murder and war | 3% | Motor accidents | 3% |

* Based on information from two church hospitals in the Northern Zone.

1976-1981, coloureds and blacks have respectively 94 and 70 percent added risk of dying from cancers compared with whites. After considerations of the quality of data have been settled, some possible explanations for this include the fact that drinking water is piped to Katatura (the black residential area of Windhoek) in Grade B asbestos piping. This is an interesting contrast to the Grade A asbestos piping used in the sewage reticulation serving the white area of Windhoek. Also, asbestos sheeting has been widely used for building houses in Katatura, with massive dust exposure for residents and no personal protection for the builders.

People classified as coloured are 230 percent more at risk of death from hypertension (high blood pressure) and stroke than are whites. Urban blacks are 50 percent more at risk from these causes than are whites. Whereas the incidence of hypertension in a living population may be related to numerous factors – including stress, inherited predisposition and diet – as a cause of death it is a different matter. With adequate health care, specifically well supervised antihypertensive therapy, deaths due to hypertension can be reduced considerably. In this light, the substantially higher death rates from hypertension among coloureds and blacks can be taken as evidence of their different access to adequate health care. The relatively low figure for blacks compared with coloureds is probably due to the different age and sex structure of the population. The coloured urban population is a relatively 'even' distribution of men and women, children and older people. Among the black urban population, a much larger proportion are young male migrant workers who are not likely to be at such high risk of hypertension. These 'dilute' the rates among blacks.

This difference in the age structure of the various skin colour groups may also explain much of the 40 percent lower risk for blacks of dying from heart disease when compared with whites. Although the standardized death rates for heart disease appear similar for whites and coloureds, it is likely that more heart disease deaths among coloured result from rheumatic heart disease than is the case among whites. Data are not available from Namibia to support this contention, but the same theme is very well documented in South Africa.

The pattern of death in urban areas as evidenced by Windhoek demonstrates thus far that blacks and coloureds carry a disproportionate burden of mortality with a large part of it being preventable. It may be worth reiterating that this profile reflects the most optimistic situation. In the rural areas the death rates are much higher, a large part of this being accounted for by deaths in the lower age groups.

## Population Growth with Industrialization

There is a belief held among whites in Namibia, and among those in favour of white domination in the country, that if black population growth were slowed down, undernutrition would not be so widespread and resources could be more effectively used. An explanation for this belief may be that resources are concentrated at present in the hands of a relatively small group of people and it is they who would benefit most from a decrease in population growth. When too many impoverished people are made to subsist off too little, strain is put on the system from which the minority benefit. For these, the logical way of easing the strain is to slow down the population

**The Rossing Uranium Mine**

growth of the majority. For most blacks and coloureds, on the other hand, adult labour is the family's only saleable asset. It is necessary to produce enough labour power for survival and since so many children die before reaching an economically active age, many must be born to ensure a family's subsistence. In fact half of all deaths among coloureds and blacks which occur under the age of sixty do so under the age of five, compared with only 5 percent among people classified as white. There is, moreover, considerably less pressure on whites to have children to provide for their old age, since they are better provided for by social services.

Malnutrition is not caused merely by inadequate food production, nor by ignorance of the value of foodstuffs. Quite simply the majority of blacks and coloureds, through deliberate social policy, can no longer produce enough food for their needs and they receive wages which are too low to make up the shortfall. This poverty is the outcome of the particular form of economic development in Namibia. The subsistence farming of all skin colour groups except whites has been militarily undermined through appropriation of land and mass removals. Economically, white monopoly over land, markets and state resources has precluded the intensification of black and coloured agriculture necessary for the support of an increasing population. Socially, the necessity for labour to migrate has disorganised families and kinship systems in rural areas to an extent that traditional support systems have all but disappeared. The white, specifically South African, domination of the country has been accompanied by an ideology of 'white customs are better'. The penetration of this ideology into food habits has undermined the traditional diet of rural dwellers and urban dwellers alike, and produced a dependence on imported foodstuffs.

In immediate terms, shortage of food makes employment necessary for survival. The relatively large proportion of people in this position means that competition for employment is fierce and consequently wages are low. Low wages, since they barely keep the worker and some of his family alive, prevent people in this position of dependence from getting out of it. Thus malnutrition is central in the production and maintenance of a cheap labour supply. Apartheid provides the legal framework for this in the form of classification by skin colour, allocation of skin colours to geographic areas ('homelands') and influx control.

The development of mining, fishing and white agriculture in Namibia produced a demand for cheap labour. Parallel to this, blacks and coloureds have been removed progressively from access to production (land and cattle). Traditional agriculture has been unable to sustain the increase in population produced by restriction/shifting of people to limited zones, and this has led to a transition from subsistence agriculture to dependence on wages from migrant labour. Today agriculture, except in the white sector, is characterized by overpopulation and low productivity.

The causes for this are manifold. First, the majority of Namibians are crowded into small sectors of land ('homelands'). Second, the South African state, through the SWA Administration, has repeatedly intervened to protect and develop white agriculture at the expense of black agriculture. Land banks and cooperatives were established to extend credit and support to white farmers. State export subsidies encouraged the production through expansion of herds (sheep and cattle), mechanization, fertilizers and irrigation. The main markets were for red meat and Karakulpelts, so much production was turned over to these. Thirdly, while the migrant labour system developed, the drainage of most able bodied men to towns meant that production in the reserves declined still further. A vicious cycle was thus set up of decreasing production, increasing impoverishment and migrant labour. Fourthly, as evident in the central north (Oshana), there are areas where the population grew without any extension of the arable frontier by irrigation. This produced a disjunction between food demands and food production which could probably have been avoided with a more even development process.

## Urbanization and Urban Divisions

In Katatura residential areas are divided on 'tribal' lines to prevent unity among black workers. Since 1979 the strategy of cultivating a black middle class, which was introduced in South Africa, has also been effective in Namibia. Houses built between 1960 and 1968 are being sold to tenants with reductions for rent paid up to the time of purchase. Pressure is put on people to purchase, rather than rent, by rent increases. In 1981, for example, rents of R18.26 were increased to R41.76 'to take account of the 9.5% inflation'.

This strategy is adding another line of cleavage between blacks in the urban areas. They are thus divided on 'tribal' lines and class lines. This state of affairs is managed from the new building for 'non-white' administration which cost several million rands. Over 25 percent of the urban population live in the eight largest towns. There are no coloured or black urban local authorities – only 'advisory boards'. Municipal power therefore rests with whites.

The high crime rate in the urban areas has health implications beyond the harm done to individuals. It effectively divides black from black and deflects aggression from the whites. It reinforces the whites' notions of their own superiority while reinforcing blacks' notions of powerlessness and inferiority. Domestic servants moving to places of security in the white residential areas have their images of black inferiority visually and materially confirmed. Thus the high crime rate in the township serves to legitimate and reinforce white rule.

For large numbers of urban migrants, the only relief from tensions and insecurities is alcohol. Among all skin colour groups in Namibia, alcoholism has reached very serious proportions. The only existing statistics are those of social workers, which do not present the alcoholism rate among whites. Some 50 percent of adults in Katatura and 80 percent of those in Khomasdal are reported to be alcoholics. Even if it is presumed that these figures are inflated by the white controlled social services, they reveal a very dire situation. Furthermore, there is no alcoholic rehabilitation centre in Namibia. Whites and coloureds are referred to South Africa. Blacks are dealt with either in the short stay psychiatric wards of the general hospitals, or sent to the 'homelands', or imprisoned.

## Occupational Health

An important aspect of occupational health in Namibia is that virtually all figures are based on employers' reports. These are extremely unlikely to reflect the situation fully, since they usually are reported as worktime lost and they provide little indication of the long term effects of the disease, or the proportion which are carried back to the reserves to manifest themselves at a later date. Unless whites are employed, it is not even necessary to have health inspectors if less than 50 workers are employed. These small industries are fairly numerous and since they rely on state health services, no data is available from them. They will, however, require special attention after independence. Likewise the work hazards in agriculture can only be alluded to rather than quantified. Figures that do exist represent the very best situation. We rely below on the relatively good data provided by the diamond mining company, Consolidated Diamond Mines. Diamond mining is the least hazardous form of mining in Namibia. Conditions are most strictly controlled – perhaps more for economic reasons than for concern about health of the workers.

Some three-quarters of a million blacks in Namibia are dependent on subsistence agriculture and contract labour to mines, farms and factories. Of these an estimated 110,000 are migrants without families. Some 40 percent of the 250,000 households have a male member in distant employment, a proportion increasing to 66 percent of all subsistence agricultural households. Blacks are effectively restricted to unskilled jobs through their inferior education, job discrimination and the lack of collective bargaining rights. Although ostensibly reformed after the strike by 15,000 migrants in December 1971 and the 'dezoning' of urban areas like Windhoek in 1978, the migrant labour system remains intact in practice.

Apart from subsistence agriculture, the main employers are white owned agriculture and mining. Most fishermen are seasonal workers from South Africa, the majority of them being coloured. Some 5,000 people are involved in fish processing in white-run factories. Mining employed 17,500 people in 1977 (20 percent white, 6 percent coloured and 74 percent black). Diamonds are mined exclusively by CDM and produce 1.6 million carats a year, near capacity output. Uranium is mined at Rossing. Copper, lead, zinc, tin, wolfram (tungsten) and lithium are processed in Tsumeb and Berg Aukas. The zinc-lead-vanadium mine at Berg Aukas was closed in 1978 due to falling metal prices. It has now been reopened after purchase by Tsumeb. There are also several sites where rocksalt is made from seawater and others where semi-precious stones are mined. Most enterprises involved in commercial agriculture have to do with stock, mostly cattle. Some 80 percent of this is exported. In industry, there are about 350 manufacturers of which 16 are export oriented (mainly fish, meat and minerals); 61 are oriented towards the regional market (mills, beverages, packing, steel engineering, mechanical workshops, paints and detergents); a further 120 are oriented towards local demand (abbatoirs, butcheries,

**Living conditions for Black workers**

bakeries, building and joineries); and a further 150 are small 'homeland projects', like pottery.

## Occupational Health Legislation

Several aspects of occupational health law are dealt with below in relation to accidents. A few comments may clarify the situation further. The Factories, Machinery and Building Work Ordinance of 1952 ('Factories Act') does not apply to mines and farms. These workers, as well as domestic servants, hotel employees, restaurant trade and construction workers are not entitled to benefits from the system of inspection, licensing and regulations established under the ordinance. Black workers from 'the north' (Ovambo) are specifically excluded from provisions of paid leave.

The Mine Workers and Mineral Ordinance essentially governs health and safety in the mines. Although inspection procedures apply to employees of all skin colour, it entrenches job discrimination through restricting control over hazardous processes to whites. Although initially this was explicitly in terms of colour of skin, it is now in terms of job grade and all the higher grades are filled with whites. The Workmans Compensation Act of 1956 enshrines the payment of lower wages on the basis of skin colour through compensating people who are injured in terms of percentage of wages. There are, in addition, separate schemes for blacks and whites. For disabilities assessed to be in excess of 30 percent, blacks are given a lump sum (at most equivalent to a few months salary for whites) whereas coloured and whites get a life pension amounting to 75 percent of earnings.

The Branches of Labour and Health are responsible for the administration of labour legislation and industrial law. Other Branches are involved to deal with water supply and pollution control and the various Branches interact in a complex way on an 'agency' basis.

## Workers on White Owned Farms

Farming is the most labour-intensive and lowest-paid sector in the Namibian economy, benefiting most from the control over labour exercised by the state. In part due to their low wages which keep families well below the poverty line and in part due to restrictive legislation, farm workers are unable to leave their employment for long enough to gain other employment. In 1970-71 the agricultural census revealed the average monthly cash income of farm labourers in Namibia was R10.5, with half that amount again being given in kind (food, clothing, housing). One third of the workforce on white owned farms are migrants, and these serve to depress the wages of resident workers and to undermine their organization. A survey of conditions on 240 farms in 1972-3 indicated the average wage had increased to R12.26 per month, but was as low as R5 per month on some of the smaller farms. Bushman women in the Gobabis area received no cash, only a blanket or skirt. In 1976, the highest wages paid by members of the SWA Agricultural Union (whites) to black workers was R27 a month for a livestock manager, while inexperienced workers received R12.50 increasing to R15 a month after 18 months service. Agricultural workers are excluded from the 1976 minimum wage regulation, mostly on the basis of the non-cash benefits. In cash terms, the highest farm wages are the same as the lowest wages in the industrial sector. The payment of wages in kind complements the effect of restrictive legislation since it means workers have little available cash and consequently little possibility to seek alternative employment.

Since the largest 'crop' in Namibia is cattle and sheep, workers on farms are very often exposed to animal-carried infections including anthrax, brucellosis, TB, leptospirosis, herpes, marburg virus, trypanosomiasis, tickbite fever and ringworm. There is no way of knowing precisely how widespread these diseases are from presently available data. There has been a dramatic increase in notified cases of anthrax and brucellosis but even these figures underestimate the real situation. It is quite possible that a constant number get it each year, and the 3 to 5 fold increase over the 5 years up to 1980 merely represents increased attention to the problem. Any survey done may declare an 'epidemic' of these occupational diseases.

Farm workers are also exposed to numerous other hazards. Accidents are by far the most common among these, but since there is no way of ensuring registration of accidents, there is no indication of just how common they are. Since farm workers do not receive compensation for injuries, there is not even this crude measure. Pesticide poisoning is a notifiable occupational disease in Namibia but virtually no cases have been reported. This bears no relation to the likely level of poisoning: to combat malaria over half a million dwellings were sprayed with DDT in 1980, and more than that in earlier years.

There is an artificial delineation between what is strictly occupational and what is 'environmental' in the approach to occupational disease in Namibia. This begins with the refusal to acknowledge the existence of families of migrant workers. It goes on to presume that subsistence farmers have no occupation: they live in malaria infested areas 'incidentally' to their occupation. It includes the notion that when a family lives in a malaria endemic area, or a shistosomiasis endemic area, it is only the formally employed members who are considered to have an occupational disease. Similarly when migrant workers get TB from conditions in their living quarters, this is considered 'environmental'. The approach hinges on the view of blacks as units of labour.

## Workers in the Mines

In 1971 the minimum wages for a black labourer underground in a Namibian mine was R8.90 per month. This compared with the average wage of a white shift boss of R375 per month. Largely prompted by events in South Africa, this minimum wage was increased dramatically to R29.12 per month by 1974 – at that time roughly one half the poverty datum level for Windhoek and the R15 per week established by the government as necessary for a man and his dependents to live 'decently'. Quite apart from how this official level institutionalizes the inequalities between skin colour groups (no whites could be expected to live decently at that level), the shortfall of mining wages demonstrates the consistently inferior position of black workers. With further 'liberalization' of wages the same stratification by race has been maintained. De Beers in 1977 claimed the average earnings of African miners was R208 per month and in 1980, R240 per month. In Tsumeb mines, wages were somewhat lower at R130 average in 1979, approximately one tenth of the average earnings for whites. A difficulty in interpretation of wage figures is that whites underground are called miners, whereas most blacks are referred to as labourers and are consequently paid much less. There is a growing tendency to separate the pay still further. In 1978 for example, the wages of blacks in general increased by 9 percent, whereas among skilled blacks the increase was 30 percent. The organization of the black miners is thus fractured by conflicting interest which limits their collective bargaining for better health conditions.

Concern has rightly been expressed at health conditions in the Rossing Uranium Mines. These workers face an increased risk of several cancers, most of which manifest themselves only after the worker leaves employment. By 1980, no black worker in Namibia had been compensated for occupational cancer. While whites working at Rossing receive regular health checks, no scheme existed to monitor the exposure of blacks to radiation or pick up the early effects. In addition, very rudimentary precautions are taken with the ore 'tailings' left after uranium oxide has been extracted. The heaps are eroded by wind and the nearby Omaruru River may be polluted. Further studies during various climatic conditions are needed to investigate this. In addition, the black and coloured mine workers live mostly in Arandis, only a few miles from the mine. Whites live over 40 miles away in the coastal town of Swakopmund. There are also very different provisions of health aid according to colour of skin. Membership of the medical aid scheme is automatic for white employees whereas blacks are only allowed to join after one year's employment and are generally not accepted unless they are in the intermediate employment category. Again this means that unskilled workers, who most probably have the heaviest exposure, have the poorest health care.

**Workers in the Diamond Fields**

Diamond workers in Namibia are probably the elite among blacks: they have a fairly thorough pre-employment screening and any with disease are sent back to the labour reserves. Data provided by the Consolidated Diamond Mines (CDM) Annual Medical Reports therefore reflect the incidence of new cases of disease.

Trends in tuberculosis (TB) over time reveal a virtual explosion of the disease. The rates between 1968 and 1980 (per 1,000 black workers that year) were: 4.07; 1.08; 4.88; 1.88; 3.21; 1.34; 1.7; 3.94; 3.49; 4.2; 7.0 and 15.8 in 1980. These figures are only for chest TB discovered while the victim is still at work. The real incidence may be twice or three times this, since many who contract the disease while at work will only produce symptoms when they return home after the end of a contract.

## Accidents

The rate of accidents while on duty in the diamond mines has also increased, more than doubling over the period. Curiously, the death rate due to accidents while on duty has declined, dropping by a factor of ten over the period. This would (initially) imply that accidents at work, although increasing in number to affect five percent of the workforce each year, are getting less serious relative to earlier years. However there has not been a notable change in work time lost due to accidents at work, the rate of shifts lost has stayed more or less constant over the years. Part of the explanation may lie in the rates of injuries sustained 'outside of work time'. These have increased meteorically over the years, more than twenty fold over the period 1968-80.

## The Politics of Occupational Accidents

Since the earliest days of mining in Namibia, occupational accidents have been defined in terms of working time lost, indicative of the priorities of employers. Most occupational accidents are not fortuitous unavoidable events, but broadly the result of defective adaptation to or inadequate control of the working environment. However unintended and unforeseen they appear to be, accidents can usually be averted by sufficient care or by technical safeguards. Seen in this light accidents are a function of the separation from the production process of those who operate it. There are several components to this. The colour bar reduces efficiency and safety by keeping blacks unskilled and allowing whites to monopolize the preferred occupations. The migrant labour system gives a 'permanently temporary' nature to black labour and, among other things, that blacks often have to accept different jobs when returning for new contracts.

Apart from worker-hours lost, which are relatively inexpensively replaced, the only cost management has to pay in Namibia is the levy to the Workmens Compensation Commission. All further costs are borne directly by the Commissioner. Moreover, management is protected from claims by injured workmen under the Workmens Compensation Act. Section Seven of this act prevents an employee taking action against an employer to recover damages in respect of an occupational injury. Section Eight allows the workman to take action against a third party responsible for the accident. Section 43 allows that where accidents do occur as a result of negligence of an employer, the workman may apply to the Workmens Compensation Commissioner for compensation. There is no substantial provision to force employers to pay for accidents which are the result of their negligence. The allowances paid out by the Commissioner are totally inadequate since they are calculated as a percentage of wages earned. This means that unskilled labourers, who have particular difficulty organizing for better working conditions and are more vulnerable to occupational accidents, receive very little compensation even if a sum is awarded. While legislation thus protects the employers agianst their own negligence, no such protection is afforded to workers. In Section 27 of the Act, if the accident is attributable to misconduct of the workman (and at the moment this rests on the decision of management) no compensation is payable unless the accident causes severe disability or death and dependents are left without income. The employer may also refuse to pay the cost of medical care in these instances of 'misconduct' of the worker.

Whereas in the diamond fields about five percent of the black workforce received work injuries in 1980, in the uranium mines at Rossing at least twice this proportion were affected. In the industrial sector surrounding Windhoek estimates range from 17 to 40 percent injured each year, depending on the source of information. On white owned farms we do not even have estimates, but the situation is likely to be still worse. The detailed rules for enforcement of protective and preventive measures in industry and mining also puts workers at an immediate disadvantage. The rules are not public documents and are enforced at the discretion of the Factories Inspectorate. Apart from the confusion of who is acting as an agency for whom and is therefore able or unable to divulge information, there are secrecy provisions in the Factories Act which are used by the Inspectorate. Workers are entitled to request an investigation into any aspect of their working conditions but are not entitled to know the outcome, nor even to know whether or not the investigation was carried out.

One explanation given by the authorities for the high accident rate in industry is the shortage of inspectors. But the problem would not be solved simply by hiring more factory inspectors. The notion that enactment of legislation produces adequate protection is itself misleading. First, the legislation has been enacted on behalf of the employers. This is true both in the context of the law discussed above, and because blacks have minimal access to the legislative process. The transitory state of migrant labour further prevents the development of skills which give them bargaining power. The second fundamental reason for the failure of legislation to decrease occupational accidents is that 'adequate protection' is not constant, but dependent on the cost of protection to the employer and the forcefulness of workers demands for protection.

## Compensation and Insurance

Workmens Compensation is one of the most simple yet effective devices available to maangement in the disorganization of labour. It is relatively cheap and it retains the initiative for management in matters concerning the work place and conditions of work. The individual approach implicit in compensation is a disincentive for unity of labour and since it occurs 'after the fact' it legitimates the conditions under which the disease or accident happened. In Namibia the racial differences in compensation policies and practices both reflect and reinforce differences at the wider economic level.

As pointed out above, very few blacks in Namibia get compensated for occupational injuries. In one of the best situations in the country, diamond mining, no compensation is given for accidents, occupational diseases or deaths – although of course there is constitutional provision for compensation to be given. Although CDM employ nearly one third of all black diamond workers in Namibia, South Africa and Botswana, none were compensated for occupational disability in the period 1973 to 1980.

During this time over one hundred black diamond workers in the other diamond fields were compensated. Taking into account the marginally lower accident rate and calculating over a ten year period 1971-1980, Namibian black diamond workers who are injured in work accidents are about twenty times less likely to be compensated than their counterparts in South Africa. This is almost certainly due to the poorer organisation of workers. Outside the diamond mining sector the situation is much worse.

## Pensions

Under each of the acts which govern pension payments, the Minister can make separate regulations for different 'classes' of people. This amounts to an approximate pension ratio of 4:2:1 for whites, coloureds and blacks respectively. A survey done in 1975 by a Turnhalle Committee found about 12 percent of the labour force eligible for pensions. In order to qualify, workers had to be in permanent posts or have had long service. The figure of 12 percent is however an inflated estimate of the situation among the rural population. Almost all of the 12 percent are in fact in the towns and almost no-one in rural areas actually receives a pension. The case can be made that with this level of insecurity in old age, it is logical for the majority of the population to try to have large families. Only in this way will they be provided for in their old age. After independence substantial resources will have to be put into social security, including pensions and free health care.

## The Case for an Occupational Base to PHC in Post-Independent Namibia

If it is accepted that production is the motor of social development, and that the struggle for control of production is the basis on which social classes are organized, then a strong argument exists for a central role to be given to occupational policies in the health sector. This necessarily vague opening comment can be reinforced from three directions. First, the majority of people in Namibia live at or below the 'bread line'. The extent to which they are able to scrape together a subsistence, their nutritional status and indeed their entire life possibilities rest on their occupations. It is scarcely possible for health status and occupation to be more closely linked than through nutrition – the availability of food.

Secondly, the division and subjugation of the Namibian people during the colonial period was exercised through employment: the colour bar, influx control, migrant labour. In the process of social reconstruction which must follow after independence, if this is to redress the inequaity of the pre-independence period, employment and the place of work should be at the centre of the reconstruction process.

Thirdly, equity through health care involves more than the relatively passive process of redistribution of resources and increasing access to health care among underprivileged groups. It also includes an active dimension whereby ordinary people play an increasing role in health care as part of their increasing determination over their own circumstances. Yet observation of the experience of many countries who have attempted to develop participation in health care nationally leads one to a sober conclusion. Health care is not necessarily the set of issues around which people mobilize most easily. This is not to say mobilization around health is undesirable, merely that it is yet to be demonstrated on a national scale. It may be that ill people do not have sufficient energy while healthy people do not have sufficient motivation. Perhaps people are less impressed with the argument that

## Estimated Occupational Exposure 1980/81

| Occupation | Estimated number of Employees | Hazards of Work |
|---|---|---|
| Large Agriculture: Supervisory | 10,500 | Accidents, pesticides, infectious |
| Semi-skilled | 25,000 | diseases from irrigation and |
| Unskilled | 75,000 | animals |
| Small Agriculture | 200,000 | Infectious diseases – endemic and from animals |
| Fishing and Processing | 8,000 | Accidents |
| Managers and Administrators | 6,000 | |
| Professionals and paraprofessionals | 25,000 | |
| Domestic Workers | 30,000 | Household solvents, obesity |
| Clerical/Secretarial | 8,500 | Solvents |
| Sales and related work | 4,750 | |
| Small Employers | 10,000 | Innumerable exposures |
| Mining and Quarrying | 36,900 | Accidents, chest disease, dermatitis |
| Transport, Delivery and Communications | 16,000 | Motor accidents |
| Motor and related industry | 7,200 | Accidents, paints (anaemia, leukemia) |
| Construction Work | 13,140 | Accidents, dust (asbestos), exposure |
| Wood Furniture | 1,000 | Cancer of nose, bronchitis, dermatitis |
| Clothes, Textiles and Leather | 1,000 | (Ammonia) eye irritation, burns, chronic bronchitis |
| Food, Drink and Tobacco | 25,500 | Numerous chemical additives |
| Printing and Paper manufacture | 1,600 | Polyneuritis, joint and kidney problems, fertility and cardiovascular |
| Glass, Cement, Bricks and Tiles | 500 | Chronic bronchitis and lung cancer, anaemic |
| Chemical Workers | 300 | Suffocation, cancers, fire, dermatitis, eye inflammation |

health care (including preventive strategies like sanitation) will improve their immediate circumstances than they are with secure employment. People probably organize more 'naturally' around occupation – whether this is homestead work, subsistence farming, industrial labour or other work – than around vaccination or sanitation. If for no other reason, they work for eight or more hours a day whereas all other health related activities probably add up to as many hours per month.

## Organizing Health Care Around Occupation

It must be said from the outset that an occupational emphasis in health care has not been adopted in any African country (or any other for that matter). It is therefore not of proven value. However, where existing practices fail to produce the required results, it is necessary to adopt new strategies which are at least conceptually cohesive. Virtually all of the technology which will be used has been tried elsewhere, and only the emphasis would be different.

The proposal is to develop primary health care practices using occupation as the focal point for organization. Occupation here refers to the everyday activity whether this is productive or otherwise (schoolchildren, subsistence agriculture, housework, child-rearing, industrial or agricultural labour, service work or unemployment). The health related interests of each of these occupational groups would be identified as the starting point. These would be discussed with each group and strategies of action formulated in each instance. In different circumstances one could expect different occupations to be a successful focus for organization (where there is an energetic and motivated teacher, schoolchildren are an appropriate starting point; where there is solid trade-union organization, that may be appropriate). Which ever works in engendering participation can provide an 'inroad' to those structures not usually presented to the health care apparatus (the family). An example here might be schoolchildren who start work among preschool children, or among the elderly in the community. Another example may be the family needs of workers in a particular sector such as agricultural.

By far the majority of health problems encountered by occupational health workers are those dealt with in the course of general health care. Apart from a few specialized subsectors (veterinary, pesticide contact, dust-induced chest diseases) the commonest occupational complaints will be infectious diseases including TB, accidents and skin problems. The basic framework for primary health care should apply to each occupational health sector, with approximately one front line health worker (part time or full time for each 200-500 people). In many circumstances it will be possible for workers to elect this health worker, for example in mines, large industrial plants, ranches, or larger agricultural estates. In other situations the level of organization may be such that an appointed health worker is required. Sometimes a member of the constituency will be incapable of carrying out the functions of a front line health worker (e.g. schools) although in these situations it will still be feasible to involve those concerned in the health process (see also section on Health Personnel).

## Special Requirements of Various Subsectors

*Mining:*

Mining has been described as an evil which is necessary for the development of the country. The people who work the mines suffer disproportionately from that evil and a post-independent health strategy should be aimed at reducing this. A first step would be to increase the social prestige of the miners. They should be regarded as the heroes of labour, receiving additional holidays and pay for the work they undertake. Secondly, provisions must be made for their families to be near them as is done in most other countries apart from southern Africa. A shorter working day with a maximal working year of 9 months will substantially decrease their exposure. Overtime should be discouraged apart from exceptional and highly supervised circumstances. Production incentive bonuses should be stopped as these encourage workers to return to the face before dust has settled and to take unnecessary risks. It is also realistic to withdraw miners from the mines irrespective of their health after a certain number of years after which time they can be placed in supervisory or subsidiary occupations – that is, guaranteed employment.

*Agriculture:*

Agricultural workers are the worst off economically and healthwise. Because there is virtually no organization among these workers it is also very difficult to know the extent of animal-related diseases, pesticide intoxication, accidents or diseases endemic to the area where they live. Before any occupational health can be contemplated in this sector, organization of the workers is necessary. Health may be a useful adjunct to this organization but on its own it is unlikely to attract the attention of workers. Front line health workers in this subsector require training in emergency treatment of accidents, diagnosis and treatment of infectious diseases including those carried by animals, and an awareness of the hazards of pesticides. This includes guidelines for safe use, treatment of acute poisoning, pest control without pesticides (integrated pest management) and the principles of measurement of the hazards of pesticides. Mobile health teams working in agricultural intensive areas ought to include someone with veterinary training. This is to present a cohesive front in interactions with agricultural workers (animal and human diseases are very closely linked). As with all other subsectors the occupation may provide an 'inroad' to make contact with the families of the workers.

*Industrial Sector:*

The main problems of this sector are those of migrant labour. There is also very fragmented organization of workers. Trade union officials should be given courses in the hazards peculiar to their work. In the bigger industries it will be possible to have elected health workers who are at least part subsidized by the health sector.

*Fishing:*

Accidents and alcoholism are the main health hazards, both of which require urgent organization of the work force and the training of front line occupational health workers.

*Domestic Workers:*

These present a particular problem because of their widespread dispersion to households throughout the towns. It may still be possible to encourage unionization and use that as a starting point for health care.

# S

# Medical and Pharmaceutical Supplies

Many developing countries experience difficulties ensuring adequate medical and pharmaceutical supplies, of appropriate types, at a cost which they can afford. The difficulties largely stem from the role of the multinational companies, particularly the giant pharmaceutical companies, which largely control world drug production. They manipulate the price structure of the industry to their own advantage and, through the promotion of brand-name products, they condition and distort the beliefs of the purchaser on the effectiveness and therapeutic value of their products.

The process of ensuring that the right drugs are available where and when they are needed is not just a matter of regulating the activities of drug companies. The general problems of underdevelopment also have to be taken into account and policies implemented to deal with ordering supplies, local compounding and packaging, the problems of distribution – particularly to outlying areas and community health workers – the construction of stores and depots, the training of staff and so forth. Newly independent countries need to develop coherent policies to deal with all these questions.

Although not presuming to make policy statements for Namibia, this section outlines some points which in practice often need to be debated and studied further. First, though, why is a pharmaceuticals and medical supplies policy of particular importance?

## The Value of a Supplies Policy

We do not know how much of the Namibian health budget goes on drugs and medical supplies, but a typical picture in underdeveloped countries is for *20-30% of health expenditure to be on pharmaceuticals alone.* This is a significant proportion and given that other health expense is largely tied to fixed commitments such as salaries, it is the drugs budget where there is usually most room for cost-cutting. This is particularly clear in the case of the smaller health centres and clinics where staff costs are cheaper than the big hospitals: drug costs in such centres can be as much as 70% or even 80% of the recurrent budget.

As mentioned in Chapter 2, procurement of medical supplies for Namibia has been through South African suppliers, with evidence of corrupt practices between health service officials and the suppliers and manufacturing companies. We can assume that the result of these constraints on a normal market mechanism is to create even higher costs than might otherwise be the case. Again, it may be through a close scrutiny of medical and pharmaceutical supplies to the service that the health budget may be rationalised.

Pharmaceutical needs will be dependent on the kind of health services provided. This is not a straightforward matter of curative services needing drugs and preventive services not. Many preventive programmes and public health strategies have pharmaceutical requirements; in a country where two of the most important disease problems are malaria and TB we have a case in point. Whatever control measures are utilised for these diseases, a therapeutic strategy for each will be an integral part of any campaign. Likewise, given that maternal and child health programmes cannot take on single-handed the struggle against poverty, supplies of dietary supplements, vitamins and minerals etc, may be a vital short-term measure. Immunisation programmes will also depend on a supply of vaccines and basic equipment (as well as a network of distribution services and storage facilities).

But even if the emphasis is to be placed on prevention, it will be essential that the curative services are seen to be effective. Very often in the development of curative work – especially curative aspects of primary health care in rural areas – the presence or absence of medicines and basic equipment is crucial to success.

Given the existing extensive non-governmental health sector (mission and private) in Namibia, a great deal of thought will be needed about supplies to this sector. Leaving the non-governmental services to procure their own supplies can seriously undermine a national policy. It also leads to duplicating functions and it reduces the government's ability to cut costs by ordering in bulk. As far as possible, a procurements policy which covers both government and non-government health services (if these are to continue) would be desirable.

A brief look at Mozambique's pharmaceutical programme might be useful. In 1975 the Frelimo government established a committee to define what medicines may be allowed in Mozambique, to write new and simpler national formularies, to publish information on the choice and use of therapeutics, and to control the health service's procurements. Private pharmacies were permitted to continue but importers were required to re-register, for a fee, all drugs that they wished to supply. They soon found that import licences were difficult to obtain for products lacking proven therapeutic value and for drugs with an unreasonably high profit margin. This combination of of measures not only earned the government about US$70,000 in fees but more importantly they reduced in a semi-voluntary manner the 13,000 products on the market to only 2,600 (down further to only 1,200 by 1980).

A National Formulary which regulates the use of therapeutics in all government services was published in 1977. It included only 640 items, not all of them drugs. It showed marked similarity to the later WHO list of 200 essential drugs, which might be the point of departure for any Namibian health service. A recent revised edition of the Mozambiquan National Formulary published in 1980 lists only 343 drugs. Mozambiquan practitioners are encouraged to comment and discuss the composition of the Formulary through the provincial and national health structures. Less extensive Formularies have also been prepared for medical assistants, medical aides and other categories of health workers – for example, community health workers (*polivalentes*) can prescribe and dispense 50 drugs.

According to health workers who were in Mozambique during the introduction of the new policies and the promotion of the National Formulary, a major reason for the government's success in establishing Frelimo's policies was the high level of political consciousness among practising doctors, both those who came from various countries as co-operantes and those who opted for Mozambiquan nationality after independence.

Where a medical establishment survives independence virtually unchanged, a strict national policy on drugs may not be so easy to introduce. In Zimbabwe, where a small-scale pharmaceutical industry grew up during sanctions, the level of pharmaceutical imports nonetheless rose dramatically at independence, from Z$10.6m in 1979 to Z$16.2m in 1981. The Ministry of Health published a proposed essential drugs list for Zimbabwe (PEDLIZ) in 1981 but there appears to have been little legislative progress to put the proposed list into the statutory Regulations. Nationalization of the local pharmaceutical industry was promised by the government, and in 1983 they bought 51% of the shares in CAPS (Central African Pharmaceutical Supplies), the largest of the local firms. Critics argue that this gives the government a stake in seeing the industry maintain its high profitability (and that measures such as these serve to underwrite private capital investment and so stabilise capitalism in the country) rather than restructure the industry to meet the needs of the people.

## The International Pharmaceutical Industry

Before moving on to consider policy formulation, it may help to summarise the major features of the international pharmaceutical industry.

1. It is *monopolistic* – there are very few firms involved.
2. It is *highly profitable* to those firms.
3. The protection given by owning *patents* plays an important role in maintaining profits.
4. *Advertising* accounts for a high proportion of drug costs.
5. Continued profit-making depends on the continued search for *new drugs*.
6. Research and development tends to be conservative, and to concentrate on the therapeutic areas which represent the *largest markets*.
7. Firms make every effort to ensure that a government is *kept in ignorance* of drug prices charged elsewhere, and they supply different information about the therapeutic use of drugs.

Providing drugs for use in refugee camps has given SWAPO much experience of the international drugs industry. Purchasing drugs by tendering, although not popular with the drug companies, is nonetheless possible and can result in huge savings, and this is already being done by SWAPO.

## Questions for a Medical and Pharmaceutical Supplies Policy

*A. What Can be Done About Procurement?*

1. Is local manufacturing possible? The secondary industrial sector in Namibia is very small, and it may be that there would be insufficient industrial support for the manufacture of drugs to be a practical proposition in the near future. Local tabletting, bottling and packaging from bulk supplies is a realistic possibility.
2. Rationalisation of purchasing procedures:
   - bulk buying on a planned basis can reduce unit costs dramatically
   - limiting the range of drugs: alternative drugs are permitted only when this is essential on medical grounds. A limited range of drugs increases the scope for bulk purchasing
   - international tendering procedures: 'shopping around' can significantly reduce costs and increase bargaining power
   - planning the purchases to cover the major health problems and health service programmes
3. Rationalising the National Formulary. Starting points for this can be the WHO List of Essential Drugs, the Mozambiquan National Formularies (1977 and 1980) and the Zimbabwean Proposed Essential Drugs List – PEDLIZ (1981). The Formulary needs to be under continuous review, with opportunities for health workers in the country to make contributions.

4. Defining each health worker's freedom to prescribe: at each level in the service, the health workers' prescribing powers need to be related to their level of training, diagnostic abilities and the working situation they are likely to be in.

5. Providing information about drugs and therapeutics from reputable sources, as an alternative to drug companies' advertising.

6. Legislating for generic name prescribing: this is crucial to operating a tendering system and is important as an educational measure to move health workers away from prescribing particular brand names.

7. Cultivating cost consciousness: health workers are better able to co-operate in rational prescribing policies if they know something about which of the drugs and formulations are expensive and which are relatively cheap.

8. Introducing nationally-approved therapeutic schemes: these may be obligatory in some cases and advisory in others. They can be very useful when health professionals come from a variety of different countries and have different prescribing 'cultures'.

9. Establishing a quality control laboratory for imported and manufactured goods: purchases of brand names and generic products need to be accompanied by quality control in Namibia as the only way of guaranteeing quality.

10. Considering what over-the-counter purchase of medicaments is to be allowed, and what products could be sold in shops other than pharmacies.

11. Placing the government in a position of sole purchaser and supplier of medicaments for the health services, including mission and private services. If this is impractical, then licensing products for import can be considered, and the criteria for granting a licence carefully defined. Regulating the prices of products, and their profit margins, may also need to be considered.

12. Taking a decision about the government's attitude to existing patent laws: for example, should Namibia import from countries which violate existing patent laws?

## B.   *Problems of Medical Supplies and Their Distribution*

1. There should always be plenty of cheap, everyday drugs or else no policy will work. Quantities need to be planned on a national basis, taking into account future activities, present needs, and the practical possibility of meeting those needs.

2. Allocations to the regions also needs planning with suitable criteria:

e.g. a combination of factors such as number of beds, number of community health workers, population size, as well as current and future
needs. Training may be needed so that regions can take resonsibility for
budgetting, costing and ordering from national stores.

3. Distributing from regional to district and local levels needs careful defi-
   nition about who is responsible for what – all too easily the supplies can
   get used up at the regional capital.

4. Planning the quantities needed and their distribution might be made
   easier if standardised supplies to a health centre or for a certain grade of
   health worker are defined.

5. At both local and regional level a system of stock-keeping and advance
   ordering may be essential, and training may be needed for this.

6. An immunisation programme involving all local health workers might
   provide the basis for a continuing service to distribute and store other
   drugs besides vaccines. A 'cold chain' – which ensures that vaccines for
   an immunization programme are kept at low temperatures from the
   suppliers through to the final users – can be the first step towards a
   more comprehensive supply network. Setting up a cold chain is the type
   of development programme which multilateral aid agencies often assist.

7. The form in which products will be distributed depends on whether
   they are being imported ready-made or whether they are being formu-
   lated and packaged at national, or even regional and local levels. In each
   case this will depend on:
   – The relative costs
   – The relative ease and cost of transport
   – Their shelf-life
   – The level of training of the person dispensing.

8. Product labelling may need careful attention: own-labelling may be useful to overcome any confusion between products from different countries, with different names and standards of labelling.

9. Local traditional remedies may be acceptable for use in the health service in some contexts: but they need to be evaluated for efficacy, safety
   and acceptability. Policies on this will depend on more general policies
   on integrating traditional healers into the health service.

## C. The Private Sector

1. Goods may need to be bought by the government from private wholesalers. These companies will be interested in making their own profits
   and they will be keen to import and sell the products with the highest
   profit margin. This may result in the promotion of expensive drugs

where cheaper ones would do, and the promotion of drugs packed for retail sale rather than cheaper packaging for bulk hospital purchase. Control of private wholesalers needs to be exercised through a drug licensing system and through limits on prices and profit margins. Monitoring of their everyday activities is useful – over-invoicing, transfer-pricing and other deceptions need to be checked.

2.  If private retailers are selling medicaments directly to the public then their activity must also be controlled: limits put on their promotion and advertising activities, monitoring of the prescription regulations etc.

3.  Selling drugs through general retail stores will also need to be controlled – in rural Mozambique, for example, five drugs can be bought across the counter. However, a network of community health workers able to prescribe and follow up a range of common treatments should make retail trade unnecessary. Community health workers are likely to have a better attitude towards the use of drugs and would be less likely to have an interest in promoting their consumption.

These points concerning a medical supplies and pharmaceutical policy only cover some of the most fundamental questions. They are largely based on other countries' experiences in controlling, or failing to control, the activities of the powerful companies who do not have the same interests as the mass of the people. These same companies will be pleased to include Namibia as one of their client countries.

# Learning the Politics of Health

The most important health workers in the world today are women. Women play a major role in family health and the prevention of illness, particularly in the nutrition, hygiene and safety of children. Without women the health of children (and probably men) would suffer far more than it would without doctors! Doctors and men, of course, can also play important roles.

In addition to women, older children are important potential health workers. Often they are the main 'caretakers' of their younger brothers and sisters. If most school-age children in underdeveloped countries learned to make and give homemade rehydration drink to their youngest brothers and sisters each time they had diarrhoea, they could do more to reduce child mortality than all the health care now provided by all the health professionals in the world.

If 'health for all' is to become a reality then we must look for ways to

☆ train dedicated volunteer health workers;
☆ make best use of resources, including human resources.

What does this mean in terms of health education and the teaching methods used by health workers? It means that:

– parents and children are the most important providers of health care, and could play an even more important role if given the opportunity to learn additional knowledge and skills.
– the services of all other health workers should be auxiliary to that of parents and children. They should have as their primary aim the upgrading of the health skills of parents and children.
– the teaching methods used for all levels of health workers, from community health workers to doctors, should as much as possible be those that work best for educating parents, children and other community members about health practices.

Equally important in the process of health education at every level is the use of teaching methods that are consistent with the goals of a just society. This means using methods that:

**People's Liberation Army of Namibia**

- help the learners and the instructors feel that they are equals, and that everyone can learn from each other.
- communicate the information and the skills in the most enjoyable, adventurous and memorable way possible.
- help people gain confidence in themselves, especially those who are more silent or have lost hope.
- build on traditional forms of learning, caring and healing.
- make the most of local resources.
- help people rediscover and take pride in their valuable customs, home remedies and native skills.
- help people work together fairly, as a group.
- encourage learners to think things through, to make their own observations and to find their own answers, rather than simply to accept what they are told.
- help people to develop problem-solving skills: to identify their problems, analyse them, and take planned action.
- help people become more self-reliant, less accepting of dependency-creating assistance.
- help people develop a joy in working together to transform their situation.

- help people to become aware of changes and obstacles to their well-being and to take organised action to overcome or avoid such dangers.
- encourage the learners to question authority.

Specific methods that incorporate these and other goals are illustrated in David Werner and Bill Bower's handbook *Helping Health Workers Learn* (see Appendix). Many of his examples have been developed by health workers in rural Mexico and have yet to be tried in Namibia.

We will now look closely at a few of the teaching methods that David Werner has found most useful in getting both health workers and villagers to analyse the problems in their communities. We have adapted them from his book and rewritten them to fit more closely the situation in Namibia. They consist of a series of learning exercises which follow the telling of a story: a story such as *Saki, the Boy Who Died of Tetanus*.

## The Story of Saki

Saki was a 7-year-old boy who died of tetanus. He lived with his mother near the small village of Outapi, 15 miles by dirt road from the town of Okahao. In Okahao there is a mission hospital staffed by a doctor and several nurses. The hospital conducts a vaccination programme and has a Land Rover. But the vaccination programme only occasionally reaches nearby villages. One year the health team began to vaccinate in Outapi, but after giving the first vaccination of the series they never returned. Perhaps they grew discouraged because many parents and children refused to co-operate. Also, the road to Outapi is very dusty and hot.

When the staff of the mission hospital failed to return to Outapi a midwife from the village went to Okahao and offered to take the vaccine to the village and complete the vaccination series. She said she knew how to inject. But the doctor refused, saying that the children's lives were in danger if the vaccines were given by people without formal training.

Three years later the boy Saki was herding his father's cattle when he stepped on a long thorn with his bare foot. Saki owned some shoes but they were broken and too worn out to repair. His father had gone to the mines to look for work and his mother farmed other people's land to earn a little money. They were too poor to buy new shoes for Saki. So he went barefoot. The boy pulled the thorn out and limped back home.

Nine days later the muscles in Saki's legs grew stiff and he had trouble opening his mouth. The next day he had spasms in which all the muscles in his body suddenly tightened and his back and neck bent backwards.

The village midwife at first recommended a herbal tea, but when the spasms got worse she suggested to Saki's mother that she take him to the mission hospital in Okahao.

The curfew prevented her taking Saki to Okahao straight away, so it was early the next morning when Saki's mother paid the bottle-store owner in Outapi to drive to Okahao in his truck. She had managed to borrow thirty rand, but the bottle-store owner charged her twelve rand for the trip. This was much higher than the usual price.

In Okahao, she and Saki waited for two hours outside the hospital. When it was finally their turn to see the doctor he immediately diagnosed the illness as tetanus. He explained that Saki was in grave danger and needed injections of tetanus antitoxin. He said that these were very expensive and, in any case, he did not have them. Saki would need to be taken to Windhoek, over 200 miles away.

Saki's mother despaired. She had barely enough money left to pay their bus fare to Windhoek. If her son died, how would she get his body back to the family graveyard in Outapi?

So she thanked the doctor, paid his modest fee, and took the afternoon bus back to Outapi. Two days later, after great suffering, Saki died.

★     ★     ★     ★     ★

WHAT CAUSED SAKI'S DEATH? This is a key question to start discussion after telling the story. The question can be approached in many ways. Here is one possibility:

*METHOD 1: The Question Game: 'BUT WHY...?'*

To help a group look at the chain of causes that led to Saki's death, play the game 'But Why...?' Everyone tries to point out different causes. Each time an answer is given, ask the question 'But Why...?' This way everyone keeps looking for more causes. If the group looks at only one area of causes but others exist, then the discussion leader may need to go back to earlier questions and rephrase them so the group explores new areas.

For example, after the STORY OF SAKI, the 'But Why...?' question game might proceed like this:

Discussion leader's question: What caused Saki's illness?
    Group's answer: Tetanus – the tetanus infection.

Q:  BUT WHY did the tetanus infect Saki and not someone else?
Group:  Because he got a thorn in his foot.

Q:  BUT WHY did that happen?
Group:  Because he was barefoot

Q:  BUT WHY was he barefoot?
Group:  Because he wasn't wearing shoes.

Q:  BUT WHY not?
Group:  They broke and his mother couldn't afford to buy new ones.

Q:  BUT WHY is his mother so poor?
Group:  Because the land is so poor, and she has to work on other people's land.

Q:  BUT WHY is their land poor?
Group:  The best land belongs to the big private farmers.

Q:  BUT WHY?
(A long discussion can follow on the history of Namibia's colonisation and the development of private ownership and wage labour.)

Q:  Let us go back a bit. What other reason is there for the tetanus to attack Saki and not someone else?
Group:  Because he was not vaccinated.

Q:  BUT WHY was he not vaccinated?
Group:  Because his village was not well covered by the vaccination team from Okahao mission hospital.

Q:  BUT WHY was the village not covered?
Group:  Because the villagers did not co-operate enough with the team when it did come to vaccinate.

Q:  What is another reason?
Group:  The doctor refused to let the midwife give vaccinations.

Q:  BUT WHY did he refuse?
Group:  Because he did not trust her. Because he thought it would be dangerous for the children.

Q:  WHY did he think that? Was he right?
(Again, a whole discussion.)

Q:  BUT not all children who get tetanus die. WHY did Saki die and others live?

Group: Perhaps it was God's will.

Q: BUT WHY Saki?
Group: Because he was not treated adequately.

Q: WHY NOT?
Group: Because the midwife tried first to treat him with herbal tea.

Q: WHY ELSE?
Group: Because the doctor in Okahao could not treat him. He wanted to send Saki to Windhoek for treatment.

Q: BUT WHY?
Group: Because he did not have the right medicine.

Q: WHY NOT?
Group: Because it is too expensive.

Q: BUT WHY is this life-saving medicine so expensive?
(A long discussion can follow. Depending on the group, it might include comments on the power and profits of the companies, etc.)

Q: BUT WHY did Saki's mother not take him to Windhoek?
Group: She did not have enough money.

Q: WHY NOT?
Group: Because the bottle store owner charged them so much to drive them to Okahao.

Q: WHY did he do that?
(A discussion on exploitation can follow.) Group: Because she was poor.

Q: BUT WHY is she so poor? (This question keeps coming up.)

         ★     ★     ★     ★     ★

## METHOD 2: *Biological Physical and Social Causes of Illness*

It may help to analyse the causes of ill-health and see how these causes relate to each other. One way of sorting them out is as follows:

BIOLOGICAL – caused by a living organism such as a virus, bacterium, parasite or fungus.

PHYSICAL – caused by some condition in the physical environment such as a thorn, or lack of sufficient water, or crowded living conditions.

SOCIAL – caused by human factors and the way people relate to each other and treat each other. Social causes can be divided into three sorts:

CULTURAL – to do with people's attitudes, customs, beliefs and schooling (or lack of schooling).

ECONOMIC – to do with money, land and resources – who has them and who does not.

POLITICAL – to do with power – who controls whom and how.

The discussion group can list the various causes of a particular illness in columns under the headings Biological, Physical and Social. For example:

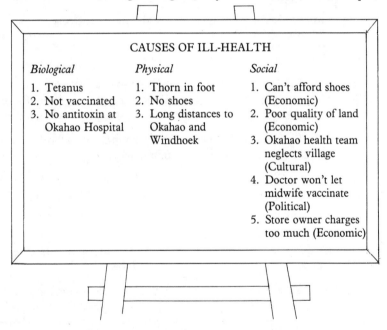

### CAUSES OF ILL-HEALTH

| Biological | Physical | Social |
|---|---|---|
| 1. Tetanus | 1. Thorn in foot | 1. Can't afford shoes (Economic) |
| 2. Not vaccinated | 2. No shoes | 2. Poor quality of land (Economic) |
| 3. No antitoxin at Okahao Hospital | 3. Long distances to Okahao and Windhoek | 3. Okahao health team neglects village (Cultural) |
| | | 4. Doctor won't let midwife vaccinate (Political) |
| | | 5. Store owner charges too much (Economic) |

As the members of the group draw up the list they will soon realise that social causes usually lie behind the biological and physical causes, and the social causes are much more numerous. It is important to focus attention on these social causes because...

... social causes are often ignored by professionals and authorities, and

... only after the social causes of ill-health have been dealt with can there be long-lasting improvements in the health of the poor.

★      ★      ★      ★      ★

*METHOD 3:*   *The Chain of Causes*

A group may get a better understanding of the chain of causes leading to illness and death if an actual chain can be made. Each time another cause is
mentioned another link is added to the chain.

A chain can be drawn on a blackboard or a large sheet of paper. Or cut out
cardboad links, and drawings of Samu and a grave. These can be hung on a
wall or fixed on a board.

The 'Chain of Causes' might begin something like this:

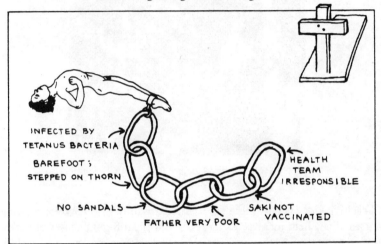

Different coloured links can be used to represent the five types of causes.
Everyone can help draw and cut out several of each sort before the game starts.

The group can form the 'Chain of Causes' as they play the game 'But Why...?' or they can do it as a review after the 'But Why...?' game. Each member of the group is given a few links. Then each time a new cause is mentioned, everyone considers whether it is biological, physical, cultural, economic or political. Whoever has the right sort of link for a particular cause can come forward and add the link to the chain.

Link by link it grows until it reaches the grave.

Here a chain is being made about
a child who died of diarrhoea.

Teaching aids such as these are useful early in health workers' training courses. They help increase awareness about the different causes of health problems and the way they relate to each other. Health workers can then use these same aids to teach groups in their communities.

NOTE: Words like *biological, physical* and *social* might be better replaced by simpler terms that people use already. For example, for *cultural, economic* and *political* simpler words such as *belief, money* and *power* could be used. And for people who can't read it is useful to represent these words with drawings and well-known symbols.

*     *     *     *     *

## METHOD 4:   *But What Can We Do?*

After analysing the causes of Saki's death, the next step is to ask the question 'What can we do?'

It is often easier to start by asking a group to consider what other people might do. So ask 'What could the people of Outapi do to help prevent the death of other children like Saki?'

Members of the group may have a wide variety of suggestions, some more realistic than others:

'Organise the community to insist that nurses from Okahao come to vaccinate the children.'

'Hold parties and take collections to raise money for poor families that need medical treatment'

'Arrange to have someone in the village trained as a health workers.'

'Start a co-operative so people share their land and everyone can afford shoes and other basic needs.'

'Try to get the authorities to make laws to redistribute the large farms and the good land.'

'Organise the poorer farmers to take over the good land that isn't being used.'

'Arrange to get loans for groups of poorer farmers so they can buy good land and farm equipment.'

'Join with workers' organisations to get changes that will put an end to big private farms and other causes of poverty.'

These are all the sorts of suggestions that have been made by villagers in discussions groups in various countries. But they are more than just suggestions. Community projects and health workers are already trying out some of these ideas!

Clearly, people in Namibia may have different ideas to the examples given. Both the suggestions people make and the way they get carried out will depend on local factors.

In some places, villagers may not be ready to make many suggestions. Or they may make only 'well-behaved' suggestions such as 'Talk to the nurses and see if they would be willing to come and vaccinate the children.' Any proposals that poor people should organise, insist on their rights, or take action to resist the abuses of those in power may seem strange or fearful to them.

Even in places where more and more people are becoming aware of the possibilities, most poor people feel there is very little they can do to change their situation.

For this reason, many community projects make the development of critical awareness a primary concern. Through special educational methods and 'group dialogues', they try to help people look at their situation more closely, realise the possibilities for changing it, and gain the self-confidence to take positive, co-operative action. This process of building social and self-awareness is the main theme of this chapter . . .

...Social change, through which the poor gain more control over the conditions that affect their well-being, is the key to 'health for all.'

*       *       *       *       *

Turning to another teaching method, not based on a 'Saki' story, let us consider one that health workers have used to help community members consider the relative importance of different local problems affecting health, and how they inter-relate.

| PROBLEM | HOW COMMON | HOW SERIOUS | HOW IMPORTANT |
|---|---|---|---|
| Babies have diarrhoea | + + + + + | + + + + | 9 |
| Children have worms | + + + + | + + | 6 |
| Children very thin | + + + + | + + + | 7 |
| Skin sores | + + + + + | + | 6 |
| Toothaches | + + | + + + | 5 |
| Chickens died | + + + | + + + | 6 |
| Too far to water | + + + + + | + + | 7 |
| Fever and chills | + + + | + + + + | 7 |
| Fathers often drunk | + + + | + + + + | |
| Crops failed | + + + | + + + + + | |
| Food in store too costly | + + + + | + + + + | |
| Heart attacks | + | + + + + | |
| Women pale and weak | + + + | + + + | |
| Problems after birth | + + | + + + + | |
| Measles | + + | + + + | |
| Common colds | + + + + + | + | |

+ not very common (or serious)
+ + somewhat common (or serious)
+ + + common (or serious)
+ + + + very common (or serious)
+ + + + + extremely common (or serious)

*METHOD 5:*   *The Importance of Different Health Problems*

Looking at health problems can be done in several ways. One way is to make a chart on a blackboard or large piece of paper. The group discusses *how common* and *how serious* they feel each problem is. They can give each problem a score, say from one to five for each column, like the diagram on page 131.

By considering how common and how serious a problem is, members of the group can get an idea of its *relative importance to the community*. To help in this, they can add up the plus marks for each problem.

Ask the group which problem appears to be most important (diarrhoea, with 9 pluses, in our example). Then which is the next most important (with 8 pluses)? And so on.

Instead of just two columns for common and serious, the group can consider four aspects of each problem:

1. How *common* is the problem in the community?
2. How *serious* are the effects on individuals, families and communities?
3. Is it *contagious*? (Does it spread to other people?)
4. Is it *chronic*? (Does it last a long time?)

Again, plus marks can be used to add up the results. More fun than just using plus marks, though, is to get everyone involved in making and using cut-out symbols:

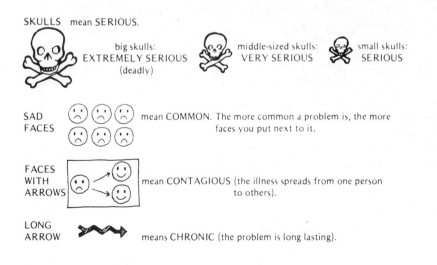

SKULLS   mean SERIOUS.

big skulls:
EXTREMELY SERIOUS
(deadly)

middle-sized skulls:
VERY SERIOUS

small skulls:
SERIOUS

SAD
FACES   mean COMMON. The more common a problem is, the more faces you put next to it.

FACES
WITH
ARROWS   mean CONTAGIOUS (the illness spreads from one person to others).

LONG
ARROW   means CHRONIC (the problem is long lasting).

These symbols can be made of flannel or soft cloth, to be used on a flannel-board. Groups usually need at least:

100 sad faces
10 of each skull
20 faces with arrows
10 of each arrow

Different colours can be used for each sort of symbol. The name of the proble·n can also be written on a strip of white cloth, or a strip of paper pinned to the board. The problems can be discussed one by one, and group members come forward and place the symbols they think fit on each problem.

The board might finish looking like this:

The group members can be encouraged to argue about how many sad faces to put next to *cough* compared to *diarrhoea,* for example, or whether *drunkenness* is contagious or not. This will get them thinking and talking about the problems in their community.

Using these methods to train health workers can lead to interesting differences of opinion. Health workers may come from different areas: some may come from hot, low-lying villages where diarrhoea, hookworm and typhoid are more common, while others come from high, cooler areas where colds, bronchitis or pneumonia are more common. Health workers soon discover how problems and needs vary from village to village.

*For those who cannot read* it is possible to use similar teaching methods, but instead of using words te group leader uses representative drawings and explains what they mean. Once they are explained people rarely forget what they mean. Here are some examples:

★     ★     ★     ★     ★

Some of these ideas may help to develop appropriate teaching and learning methods for health education in Namibia. Of course, only first-hand experience will lead to the best suggestions and ideas.

There are a large range of educational materials and publications avalable. In the Appendix we give some further ideas: more reading that can be done and aid agencies and organisations that can be approached to give material on health in developing countries.

Of course, these learning methods don't only apply to developing countries – they can be used wherever appropriate to raise discussions about health and health services, in industrialised countries too. The story of Saki might need some changes, but with a little imagination this can soon be done.

Some things just have to be created on the spot, though. Some groups of health workers in Nicaragua have made a puppet show which they take around the villages, and have written a very realistic play with individual spoken parts:

The Farm People's Theater
presents:
"THE IMPORTANCE
OF BREAST FEEDING
AND NOT BOTTLE FEEDING"

There was also a street theatre acted by a group of community health workers as part of the national vaccination campaign in 1982, and called:

The Measles Monster

The importance of this kind of theatre depends on audience participation. Children in the street, especially, can become actively and excitedly involved. There is no stage, the actors simply start by standing in the street with their masks on. Soon a crowd gathers and a narrator with a loudspeaker starts to provide an explanation while the actors mime the play...

# Concluding points

Each part of this book looks at health in its own particular way. Chapters two and three take occupied Namibia as their starting point and discuss the heritage that an Independent Namibia will face, with its gross inequities and divisions between races, classes and sexes.

In the following two chapters, four and five, the main political principles are considered: the political nature of health, the need to decentralise control over health resources, the need to consider the political orientation of health workers and the need to continue the struggle long after independence is achieved. These principles are born of experience – and chapter five goes to some length to show how other countries have re-shaped their health services and what has followed.

Chapters six, seven and eight take a range of topics that normally concern a health authority in a developing country. The topics are looked at in various different ways, reflecting both the variety of the material available at the International Seminar (which formed the basis for this book) and also the different perceptions that individual contributors have about how best they can offer support and solidarity to Namibians in struggle. In some sections the approach has been to ask a series of pertinent questions which may assist policy implementers as they draw up their programmes. In other sections some answers are presented, usually based on the experiences of health workers from developing countries, as a possible guide for Namibia. These are all offered in the spirit of support. The contributors all appreciate how Namibia's unfolding history will in practice be very different to that of Zimbabwe or Mozambique, let alone that of Mexico or Nineteenth Century Britain.

Even to draw lessons from countries in the region with similar social features such as Mozambique and Zimbabwe begs a lot of questions. Mozambique and Zimbabwe are themselves very different from each other both in their colonial history and now, too, in the policies of their independent governments. Mozambique's health budget is over 10% of total government expenditure while Zimbabwe's is little more than half that proportion: about 6% of government expenditure is on health. But in contrast Mozambique can afford little more than US$6 per person for a year's health, while Zimbabwe spends over US$16 per person, not counting the costs borne by the religious missions and the extensive private health services. Both countries have one thing in common which might be held in mind for Namibia: since independence the amount spent by each government on health has trebled, within seven years for Mozambique and within four years for Zimbabwe.

These differences in health expenditure reflect the different economic strengths of the two countries. Where does Namibia fit in? Like Zimbabwe (but unlike Mozambique), Namibia is a relatively wealthy country. Its Gross Domestic Product was estimated at some US$1.1bn in 1977[1] – equivalent to about $900 per person (Zimbabwe's figure was about $350 per person that year and is over $500 now, Mozambique's is under $300 now). But Namibia's GDP does not all stay in Namibia. Between a third and a half of it is paid out as profits and dividends to foreign investors and wages to expatriate workers.[2] And, as we know, most of the remaining wealth is distributed to a small section of the population. Actual per capita income was nearer $125 for blacks and $3,000 for whites.[3]

All this amounts to saying that the money is there – but to redistribute it will require a major upheaval in the economic system, both equalising the wages and services for all sections of the population, and drastically limiting the amount of wealth being remitted abroad. This might sound like a recipe for the sort of economic collapse Mozambique experienced at independence, but this is unlikely. Namibia's resources cannot be carried over the border in a truck during the night and there is little chance that the fixed capital equipment will be sabotaged or left to decay when such strategically valuable minerals are at stake. And the mining companies have been warned: in 1974 the UN Council for Namibia, as the legal authority over the country, decreed that any natural resources taken from Namibia without the Council's consent were liable to be seized and forfeited and that any person or corporation contravening the decree might be held liable for damages by the future government of an independent Namibia. Although the UN lacks effective power to implement this decree, foreign companies continuing to exploit the resources are acting in violation of international law.[4]

Potentially, then, Namibia is in a fortunate position. Its future health ministry may not have to work on a shoe-string budget nor have to compete with other ministries for essential resources.

The money should be there. The independent government has the support of the international community, as expressed through the UN, to confront the multinational companies and so reclaim the country's wealth.

It also has the support of the international community of health workers, as expressed through this book, to confront the old services and so reclaim the people's health.

★     ★     ★     ★     ★

## References

1  G & S Cronje, *The Workers of Namibia*, International Defence and Aid Fund: London, 1979 p 16.
2  *Ibid* p 15.
3  *Ibid* p 43.
4  *Namibia – The Facts*, International Defence and Aid Fund: London, 1980 p 26.

# Resources and further reading

## Organisations

All the following organisations have an interest in what is happening in Namibia and in their various ways are supporting the struggle for change. Each of them can be written to for more information about their activities (you might ask for a sample copy of their regular journal or a copy of their latest Annual Report) along with a list of their current publications.

*SWAPO of Namibia*
Overseas offices include: P O Box 194, London N5 1LW, U.K.

Founded in 1960, the South West African People's Organisation is recognised as the authentic representative of the Namibian people by the United Nations General Assembly, and as the liberation movement of the Namibian people by the Organisation of African Unity, as well as being recognised diplomatically by the Non-Aligned countries and most governments – with the exception of Britain and the major Western trading partners of South Africa. Although SWAPO has not been formally banned by South Africa, arrests and harassment of members and frequent police raids on the Windhoek office has made internal political organisation increasingly difficult and dangerous. In 1966 SWAPO adopted a policy of armed struggle against the South African occupation of Namibia with the formation of the *People's Liberation Army of Namibia* (PLAN). SWAPO also operates extensive educational and relief programmes for Namibian refugees in Angolan and Zambian camps, setting up self-help schemes, schools and health centres.

*African National Congress of South Africa*
Overseas offices include: P O Box 38, 28 Penton St, London N1 9PR, UK.

The ANC was founded in 1912 and in June 1955 the Freedom Charter was drawn up and remains the basic statement of the liberation movement. *Umkhonto we Sizwe* (MK) is the armed wing of the ANC, formed in 1961, and both the ANC and MK are banned in South Africa. The ANC is responsible for caring for many exiled South African refugees in neighbouring countries and has established projects such as the Solomon Mahlangu Freedom College in Tanzania. The ANC is recognised as the libration movement of the South African people by the United Nations, the Organisation for African Unity, the Non-Aligned Countries, and many other governments.

*Namibia Support Committee*
P O Box 16, London NW5 2LW, U.K.

The *Namibia Support Committee* (NSC) is a solidarity organisation concerned with distributing information and organising campaigns for the liberation of Namibia, acting in support of the South West Africa People's Organisation (SWAPO). The NSC is officially recognised by the United Nations Council for Namibia as a non-governmental organisation working in support of United Nations policy on Namibia. Write to the NSC for information of its activities, including information about the following campaigns:

The *Campaign Against the Namibia Uranium Contract* (CANUC) is active against the continuing purchase by the British government and the Central Electricity Generating Board of shipments of uranium oxide from Namibia, shipments declared illegal by the UN Council for Namibia.

The *SWAPO Womens Solidarity Campaign* (SWSC) promotes understanding of the nature of Namibian women's oppression and their role in the liberation struggle, and campaigns for material aid, for literacy projects, for the release of women political prisoners and in the Peace Movement.

The Namibia Support Committee *Health Collective* has been sending material aid to SWAPO's Department of Health since 1977, including over 200 medical kits, relief supplies, clothing, vehicles and educational material, as well as liaising with other organisations which support SWAPO to send items such as water pumps, hand tools and dentist kits. The Health Collective also works to promote awareness of the health needs of Namibians with conferences and meetings throughout Britain, and with publications and posters.

*International Defence and Aid Fund for Southern Africa*
Canon Collins House, 64 Essex Road, London N1 8LR, U.K.

The *International Defence and Aid Fund* (IDAF) is a humanitarian organisation dedicated to the achievement of free, democratic, non-racial societies throughout Southern Africa, and in particular working to (1) aid, defend and rehabilitate the victims of unjust legislation and oppressive and arbitrary procedures, (2) to support their families and dependents, and (3) to keep the conscience of the world alive to the issues at stake. IDAF runs a comprehensive information service on Southern African affairs including visual documentation, and the publication of a news bulletin, pamphlets and books.

The *IDAF Book Centre*, stocking a range of material on Southern Africa, is open Mondays to Fridays at Canon Collins House, 64 Essex Road, London N1, U.K.

National committees affiliated to IDAF work to assist refugees from Southern Africa, promote information about apartheid and related issues, and help to raise money for the aims and objects of IDAF. The following countries have national committees: Britain, Canada, India, Ireland, Netherlands, New Zealand, Norway, Sweden, United States of America. The *British Defence and Aid Fund* shares the same address as IDAF.

## *Anti-Apartheid Movement*
113 Mandela Street, London NW1 0DW, U.K.

The *Anti-Apartheid Movement* (AAM) was founded in 1959 to campaign against all forms of collaboration with apartheid: challenging the policies of successive British governments which refuse to confront South Africa; exposing the multinational companies which work with and profit from apartheid; educating and organising to arouse public opinion about events in Southern Africa; campaigning in solidarity with political prisoners and detainees; and mobilising support for the southern African liberation movements. The AAM has over 60 local groups around Britain.

AAM has several off-shoots, including the *Anti-Apartheid Health Committee*, which aims to inform people in Britain on the effects on health of South Africa's apartheid system and break the links between Britain and South Africa in the health field. Contact the AAHC through the AAM's address above.

## *Catholic Institute for International Relations*
22 Coleman Fields, London N1 7AF, U.K.

The *Catholic Institute for International Relations* (CIIR) is an independent Catholic organisation working to promote a better understanding of international justice and peace issues. It is a centre for information and education on international questions, particularly relating to Latin America, Southern Africa and general development issues. CIIR publishes material in the UK as part of its education programme, and it recruits skilled/qualified people for service overseas in conjunction with the *British Volunteer Programme*.

*Namibia Refugee Project*
22 Coleman Fields, London N1 7AF, U.K.

The main concern of the *Namibia Refugee Project* (NRP) is to assist with the training of Namibians from the refugee camps so that the exiled communities can be more self-reliant in meeting their needs. Training has included shoe-making, literacy, building and water management, and a course in Development Studies, nearly all training being held away from the camps because of the danger of South African raids. The NRP has assisted in setting up workshops in the camps and supplies books for use in Namibian study projects in Angola. The NRP intends to increase its publicity and information work in Britain to raise awareness of the suffering of the Namibian people.

*Liberation*
313/5 Caledonian Road, London N1, U.K.

*Liberation* has a history of over 50 years of campaigning in Britain against colonialism and imperialism, and has worked to support liberation struggles throughout the underdeveloped world. Meetings and conferences are regularly organised and Liberation has also turned its attention to education to combat racism in Britain.

## Development Agencies

Many of the non-governmental agencies concerned with health and under-development have an interest in Southern Africa and Namibia. A selection of agencies in Britain follows (please note that many of them have local branches which welcome public interest in their work):

*War on Want*
467 Caledonian Road, London N7 9BE.

*Oxfam*
274 Banbury Road, Oxford OX2 7DZ.

*International Voluntary Service*
53 Regent Road, Leicester LE1 6YL.

*Appropriate Health Resources and Technologies Action Group*
85 Marylebone High Street, London W1.

*Third World First*
232 Cowley Road, Oxford OX4 1UH.

*Christian Aid*
240 Ferndale Road, London SW9.

*Catholic Fund for Overseas Development (CAFOD)*
2 Garden Close, Stockwell Road, London SW9 9TY)

*International Campaign on Abortion Sterilisation and Contraception*
374 Grays Inn Road, London WC1.

*Institute of Development Studies*
University of Sussex, Brighton, Sussex.

*Save the Children Fund*
Mary Datchelor House, Camberwell Grove, London SE5.

*Teaching Aids at Low Cost* and *Tropical Child Health Unit*
Institute of Child Health, 30 Guilford Street, London WC1N 1EH.

*World University Service (UK)*
20 Compton Terrace, London N1.

*Voluntary Service Overseas*
9 Belgrave Square, London SW1.


**Overseas Organisations**

There are also many overseas agencies, both multilateral and non-governmental, which have interests in Namibia and are working for change in Southern Africa. A selection follows:

*United Nations Council for Namibia*
UN Building, New York, NY 10017, USA.

*United Nations Institute for Namibia*
Box 33811, Lusaka, Zambia.

*United Nations Centre Against Apartheid*
United Nations, New York, NY 10017, USA.

*United Nations High Commission for Refugees*
Palais des Nations, CH-1211 Geneva, Switzerland.

*World Health Organisation*
Avenue Appia, 1211 Geneva 27, Switzerland.

*Hesperian Foundation (USA)*
1692 Palo Alto, California 94302, USA.

*Africa Group (Sweden)*
Box 5847, 10248 Stockholm, Sweden.

*American Committee on Africa (USA)*
198 Broadway, New York, NY 10038, USA.

*Namibia Association (Norway)*
N-2400 Elverum, Norway.

*Holland Committee on Southern Africa (Netherlands)*
Oudezijds Achterburgwal 173, 1012 DJ Amsterdam, Netherlands.

*Anti-Apartheid (Netherlands)*
Laubiergracht 116, Amsterdam, Netherlands

*Anti-Apartheid (W. Germany)*
luchterstrasse 14, 53 Bonn 1, W. Germany.

*Anti-Apartheid (Ireland)*
20 Beechpark Road, Foxrock, Co Dublin, Eire.

*Anti-Apartheid (Japan)*
c/o A. Kusuhara, 1072 Okamura, Osogo-ku Yokohama, Japan 235.

*Anti-Apartheid (New Zealand)*
P.O. Box 9154, Wellington, New Zealand.

*Anti-Apartheid (Portugal)*
Rua Artilharia Um, 105, 3 Lisbon, Portugal.

*Africa Committee (Finland)*
Bulevardi 13A9 Helsinki, Finland.

*Committee Against Colonialism and Apartheid (Belgium)*
Avenue Beau 14, 1410 Waterloo, Belgium.

*Southern Africa Committee (Denmark)*
Hejrevej 38, DK-2400 Copenhagen, Denmark.

*World University Service (Denmark)*
Gothersgade 151, DK-1123, Copenhagen, Denmark.

*Oxfam (Canada)*
251 Laurier Avenue West, Suite 301, Ottawa, Canada K1P 5J6.

*La Service Universitaire Canadien Outre-Mer (Canada)*
6839 rue Drolet, Montreal, Quebec, Canada H2S 2T1.

*Canadian University Service Overseas (Canada)*
151 Slater Street, Ottawa, Canada K1P 5H5.

*Socialist Solidarity (Belgium)*
Legrandlaan 65, 1050 Brussels, Belgium.

*Aktie Kommittee Zuid Afrika (Belgium)*
Maria Teresiastr 93, Leuven (3000), Belgium

*French Anti-Apartheid*
46 Rue de Vaugirard, 75006 Paris, France

*CIDMAA (Canada)*
3738, rue St-Domonique, Montréal, Québec, Canada H2X 2X9

## Publications

Many of the organisations we have mentioned above produce material about their own work and about campaigns in which they are involved. Here are some examples from the main British organisations concerned with Southern Africa:

### Namibia Support Committee
P.O. Box 16, London NW5 2LW.

*Namibia News Briefing* (monthly) and *Action on Namibia* publicaitons:
  Individual – UK £6pa; overseas £8pa; airmail £12pa
  Institutions – UK £8pa; overseas £12pa; airmail £15pa.
Send SAE for list of other publications and campaign leaflets, posters, badges, cards, records and films.

### SWAPO
P O Box 194, London N5 1LW.

*SWAPO: An Historical Profile*, 50p.
*SWAPO: Constitution*, 20p.
*Namibia Political Prisoners*, 50p.
SWAPO Information & Publicity Dept *To Be Born a Nation* published by Zed Press, 1981, £4.95.
*The Combatant*, monthly bulletin of the People's Liberation Army £6pa (UK); £8pa (Europe); £10pa (elsewhere).
*SWAPO Information Bulletin* monthly bulletin of SWAPO Dept of Information and Publicity, £6pa (UK); £8pa (Europe); £10pa (elsewhere).
*Namibia Youth*, bimonthly bulletin of SWAPO Youth League, £6pa (UK); £8pa (Europe); £10pa (elsewhere).
*Namibia Today* monthly, £6 pa (UK), £8 pa (Europe), £10 pa (elsewhere).
*SWAPO Information and Comment* monthly press digest and comments by SWAPO-UK office, £6 pa (UK), £8 pa (Europe), £10 pa (elsewhere).

### International Defence and Aid Fund for Southern Africa
IDAF Publications, Canon Collins House, 64 Essex Road, London N1 8LR.

*Focus*, IDAF bi-monthly bulletin, £3 pa (UK), £5 pa (overseas).
A. Seedat *Crippling a Nation: Health in Apartheid South Africa* 1984, £3.
*Namibia – The Facts*, 1980, £1.50p.
G and S Cronje *The Workers of Namibia* 1979, £1.50p.
B König *Namibia: The Ravages of War* 1983, £1.50p.
*To Honour Womens Day: Profiles of Leading Women in the South African and Namibian Liberation Struggles*, 1981, £1.
*Children of Namibia: Growing up under Apartheid*, Briefing Paper No 10, 1984.
Poster display: *Namibia In Struggle: A Portable Exhibition of Photographs*.

**Anti-Apartheid Movement**
13 Mandela St, London NW1 0DW.

*Anti-Apartheid News* £4.50 pa (£6.50 pa overseas airmail).
*Health and Liberation* Bulletin of the Anti-Apartheid Health Committee, £2 pa.

**The Catholic Institute for International Relations**
22 Coleman Fields, London N1 7AF.

J Ellis *Elections in Namibia* published with the British Council of Churches (BCC) 1979, 50p.
*A Future for Namibia*
   No 1: *Namibia in the 80s* published with the BCC, 1981, £1.
   No 2: R Moorsom *Transforming a Wasted Land* 1982, £2.95p.
   No 3: *Mines and Independence*, 1983, £2.95p.
   No 4: J Ellis *Education, Repression and Liberation: Namibia* (with the World University Service UK), 1984, £2.95p.
   No 5: R Moorsom *Exploiting the Sea* 1984, £2.95p.
*From Rhodesia to Zimbabwe* Nos. 1 to 9, particularly
   No 7: J Gilmurray, R Riddell & D Sanders *The Struggle for Health* 1979, 50p. and
   No 2: R Riddell *The Land Question* 1978, 40p.

**United Nations Council for Namibia**
UN Building, New York, NY 10017, USA.

*Namibia Bulletin* quarterly, including information on UN activities on Namibia.
Periodic reports including *Report on Social Conditions in Namibia* (A/AC.131/L.52), 1977, which includes health, education and housing

**Other Recommended Publications**

Most of the publications suggested above can help to tell you about what is happening in Namibia and Southern Africa. Besides these publications there is a vast wealth of material which can be purchased (or ordered through your library) about health and underdevelopment more generally, of which we can give only a small selection:

D Werner *Where There Is No Doctor* Hesperian Foundation, California, 1977.
D Werner and B Bower *Helping Health Workers Learn* Hesperian Foundation, California, 1982.
*Primary Health Care in Developing Countries: A guide to resources in the UK* Appropriate Health Resources and Technologies Action Group, London, 1982.
*Global Strategy for Health for All by the Year 2000*, WHO, Geneva, 1981.
D Morley, J Rohde and G Williams (eds) *Practising Health for All*, Oxford University Press, Oxford, 1983.
*The Political Economy of Health* by L Doyal and I Pennell, Pluto Press, London, 1979.
V Navarro (ed.) *Imperialism, Health and Medicine* Pluto Press, London, 1982.
M Muller *The Health of Nations: A North-South Investigation* Faber & Faber, London, 1982.
E de Kadt and M Segall (eds) *Health, Society and Politics* Institute of Development Studies Bulletin Volume 14, no. 4, IDS Publications, Brighton, Sussex, 1983.

G Walt and A Melamed (eds) *Mozambique: Towards a People's Health Service* Zed Books: London, 1984.
*Health Links*, Third World First, Oxford, 1981.
J Horn *Away With All Pests* Hamlyn, London, 1969.


*Women and Health*

N S Hishongwa *Women of Namibia: The Changing Role of Namibia Women from Traditional Pre-colonialist Times to the Present* By & Bygd, Stockholm, 1983.
*Women's Work – Women's Lives*, Third World First, Oxford, 1983.
*Training Course for Health Clinicians (Women's Health)* International Women's Health Coalition (1611 Connecticut Avenue NW, Washington DC 20009, USA), Washington, 1981.


*Water and Sanitation*

U Winblad and W Kilama *Sanitation Without Water* Swedish International Development Authority, Stockholm, 1980.
*World Bank Research in Water Supply and Sanitation: A Survey of Publications* free from the World Bank European Office, 66 Avenue d'Iena, 75116 Paris, France.


*Maternal and Child Health*

M King, F King and S Martodipoero *Primary Child Care A Manual for Health Workers* Oxford University Press (with WHO), Oxford, 1978.
D Morley *Paediatric Priorities in the Developing World* Butterworth, London, 1973.
D Morley and M Woodland *See How They Grow: Monitoring Child Growth for Appropriate Health Care in Developing Countries* Macmillan, London, 1979.
A Aarons, H Hawes, J Gayton and C Barker *Child-to-Child* Macmillan, London 1979.
A Chetley *The Baby Killer Scandal* War on Want, London, 1979.
M Williams *The Training of Traditional Birth Attendants* Catholic Institute for International Relations, London 1981.
*A TBA Trainer's Kit* from WHO, 1211 Geneva 27, Switzerland


*Nutrition and Underdevelopment*

J Waterlow and P Payne *The Protein Gap* in *Nature* volume 258, no. 5531, pp 113-117, London.
T Jackson and D Eade *Against the Grain: The Dilemma of Project Food Aid* Oxfam, Oxford, 1982.
C Tudge *The Famine Business* Penguin, London, 1979.
S George *How The Other Half Dies: the Real Reason for World Hunger* Penguin, London, 1976.
S George *Food for Beginners* Writers and Readers Co-op, London, 1983.
R N Taylor *Whose Land Is It Anyway?* Turnstile Press, London, 1982.
K Shack (ed.) *Teaching Nutrition in Developing Countries* Meals for Millions Foundation, Davis, California, 1979.

*Oral Health*

M Dickson *Where There is no Dentist* Hesperian Foundation, California, 1983.
*Assisting Dental Education and Dental Public Health in Developing Countries: A Symposium* Appropriate Health Resources and Technologies Action Group (AHRTAG), London, 1981.
*The Planning and Development of Educational Programmes for Oral Health Personnel*, WHO, Geneva, 1984.
*Planning Oral Health Services*, WHO, Geneva, 1980.
*Oral Health Surveys*, WHO, Geneva, 1977.
*Common Oral Diseases: Prevention and Emergency Care—A Manual for Teachers* WHO, Geneva, 1982.

*Rehabilitation*

O Shirley (ed.) *A Cry For Health: Poverty and Disability in the Third World* published jointly by the Third World Group for Disabled People and the Appropriate Health Resources and Technologies Action Group, London, 1983.
D Caston and J Thompson *Low Cost Aids* Appropriate Health Resources and Technologies Action Group, London, 1982.
D Caston and J Thompson *Low Cost Physiotherapy Aids* Appropriate Health Resources and Technologies Action Group, London, 1982.
D Caston and J Thompson *How to Make Hand Grips* Appropriate Health Resources and Technologies Action Group, London, 1984.
E Helander, P Mendis and G Nelson *Training the Disabled in the Community* WHO, Geneva, 1983.

*Pharmaceutical Supplies*

*The Selection of Essential Drugs* Technical Report Series Nos. 615 (1977) and 641 (1979), WHO, Geneva.
D Melrose *Bitter Pills: Medicines and the Third World Poor* Oxfam, Oxford, 1982.
H Martins *Pharmaceutical Policy in Independent Mozambique: The First Years, and*
S J Patel *Third World Initiatives on Pharmaceuticals: A Documentation for the Record Health, Society & Politics*, IDS Bulletin 14, No 4, IDS Publications, Brighton, Sussex, 1983.
C Medaway and B Freese *Drug Diplomacy* Social Audit, London, 1982.
*Who Needs the Drug Companies?* Haslemere Group, War on Want and Third World First, London, 1976.
J Elford *How to Look After a Refrigerator* Appropriate Health Resources and Technologies Action Group, London 1983.
A Battersby *How to Look After a Health Centre Store* Appropriate Health Resources and Technologies Action Group, London 1983.
E Sabin and W Stinson *Immunizations* Primary Health Care Issues, Series I, No 2; American Public Health Association/International Health Programs, Washington, 1981.

*Newsletters and Journals*

There are hundreds of periodicals concerned with health and development. Many of these are expensive and academic. Some of them are aimed at doctors and specialist medical staff. Yet it is often the more isolated and less qualified health worker who is in most need of being kept in regular touch with developments in health elsewhere in the world. We list below a short list of newsletters and journals which are available *free of charge* to health workers in developing countries (a more extensive list may be consulted at AHRTAG, 85 Marylebone High Street, London W1M 3DE, UK):

*African Health* Business Press Ltd, Oakfield House, Perrymount Rd, Haywards Heath, West Sussex RH16 3DH, UK.

*Aids for Living* (rehabilitation aids) AHRTAG, 85 Marylebone High Street, London W1M 3DE, UK.

*Contact* Christian Medical Commission, Route de Ferney, 1211 Geneva 20, Switzerland.

*Decade Watch* (water and sanitation decade) UNDP Division of Information, One UN Plaza, New York, NY 10017, USA.

*Dental Health Newsletter* AHRTAG, 85 Marylebone High Street, London W1M 3DE, UK.

*Diarrhoea Dialogue* AHRTAG, 85 Marylebone High Street, London W1M 3DE, UK.

*Food and Nutrition* Distribution and Sales Section, FAO, 00100 Rome, Italy.

*Future* (children's issues) UNICEF, UNICEF House, 73 Lodi Estate, New Delhi 110003, India.

*Glimpse* International Centre for Diarrhoea Disease Research, GPO 128, Dhaka 2, Bangladesh.

*Ideas and Action* (development issues) FAO, 00100 Rome, Italy.

*International Rehabilitation Review* International Society for Rehabilitation of the Disabled, 432 Park Avenue, New York, NY 10016, USA.

*IRC Newsletter* International Reference Centre for Community Water Supply, P O Box 5500, 2800 HM Rijswijk, Netherlands.

*IRCWD News* (sanitation) International Reference Centre for Waste Disposal, Uberlandstrasse 133, CH 8600 Dubendorf, Switzerland.

*L.I.F.E. Newsletter* (nutrition) League for International Food Education, Suite 915, 15th Street NW, Washington DC 20005, USA.

*Mothers and Children* the American Public Health Association/International Health Programs, 1015 15th Street NW, Washington DC 20005, USA.

*NFE/WID Exchange* (non-formal education, and women in development) Agriculture Education Department, UPLB CA College, Laguma 3720, Philippines.

*Rural Eye Health* Department of Preventive Medicine, Institute of Opthalmology, 27-29 Cayton Street, London EC1V 9EJ, UK.

*UNICEF News* (child health) Information Division, UNICEF, New York, NY 10017, USA.

*Waterfront* UNICEF Drinking Water Program, 866 UN Plaza, Room A415, New York, NY 10017, USA.

*World Health* WHO, Avenue Appia, 1211 Geneva 27, Switzerland.

# INDEX

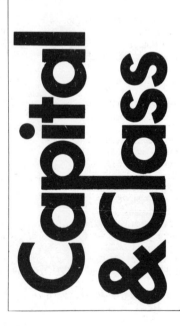

# A Future for Namibia

A series which addresses the fundamental problems of the Namibian economy.

## 1 Namibia in the 1980s

*1981  0 904393 58 5  84pp  £1*

'does much to clarify the decisions which must be made by South Africa, SWAPO and Western governments' *Guardian*

## 2 Transforming a Wasted Land
### by Richard Moorsom

*1982  0 904393 85 2  114pp with maps and tables  £2.95*

'a well written book, taking a hard look at future possibilities' *Overseas Development*

'uses a wealth of research material to describe how colonial agricultural policies and South Africa's illegal occupation of Namibia have led to impoverishment' *The Herald,* Zimbabwe

'Richard Moorsom does an excellent job in drawing together the natural, historical, economic and administrative threads in this short, sad story.' *International Agricultural Development*

## 3 Mines and Independence

*1983  0 904393 77 1  155pp with maps and tables  £2.95*

'provides an excellent overview of Namibia's mineral wealth and the opportunities and problems which SWAPO will face when freedom finally comes' *New Statesman*

'an impressively researched new report on the future of Namibia's mining industry' *Africa Now*